T0361651

Byron Wien was a friend and colleague for many decades. I will always be grateful to him for serving as interlocutor on my first memoir in 1996. For many years, I hosted his Ten Surprises lunch at my home on Long Island, where he dispensed much wisdom and original thinking, which I miss to this day.

—GEORGE SOROS
Chair, Soros Fund Management

Byron's uncanny knack to peer around corners was on full display during our twenty-one-year partnership at Morgan Stanley. His lessons are an enduring testament to what he brought to Wall Street and to those of us who were fortunate to share in his extraordinary journey. *Stay at Risk and Live Forever* keeps Byron's special spark alive for all to share.

—STEPHEN ROACH
Yale University, former chief economist and Asia chair, Morgan Stanley

Byron's intellectual curiosity, coupled with some quick humor and a healthy dose of humility, differentiated him like no other on Wall Street. He was the master of bringing ideas and capital together. Of all Byron's achievements, though, his Life Lessons will shape his legacy. This book offers valuable insights into these lessons, providing practical wisdom for readers' personal and professional lives.

—HENRY H. McVEY
Partner, chief investment officer, KKR's Balance Sheet

Byron Wien was an icon in our industry. He had a special ability to focus in on the key issues facing the market at various times and was especially talented in drawing others into the conversation with worthwhile observations. He did this in a most friendly manner and was liked and respected by all who dealt with him.

—LEE COOPERMAN
Chairman and CEO, Omega Advisors

Byron never ceased to amaze me, and he raised the bar yet again with this remarkable memoir. This book is a true page-turner, brimming with compelling and practical insights. I enthusiastically recommend it to all, as I'm certain you'll find many valuable lessons that will contribute to your personal growth.

—EDWARD HYMAN
Chairman, Evercore ISI; vice chairman, Evercore

Many people have said great things about Byron. However, the one characteristic of Byron that is often missed is his very strong personality.

Over the years, I have enjoyed attending his summer luncheons in the Hamptons and watching Byron manifest his strong personality, jousting with the billionaires (including myself) who were in attendance. Most of these billionaires have very strong personalities of their own and are not afraid to share beliefs, but Byron ruled the luncheon conversations completely. In his quiet and direct way, he showed no compunction in telling attendees when they had spoken long enough—or, in other words, to "shut up." It was fun to hear him say in his "Byronesque" way: *get rid of the cell phone.*

I always thought we needed someone like Byron in Washington, but he was too smart to go there.

—CARL ICAHN
Chairman, Icahn Enterprises

STAY AT RISK
AND
LIVE FOREVER

BYRON WIEN AND TAYLOR BECKER

STAY AT RISK AND LIVE FOREVER

LESSONS FROM A LIFE *of* CURIOSITY, GRIT, AND REINVENTION

Advantage | Books

Published by Advantage Books, Charleston, South Carolina.
An imprint of Advantage Media.

ADVANTAGE is a registered trademark, and the Advantage colophon is a trademark of Advantage Media Group, Inc.

Printed in the United States of America.

10 9 8 7 6 5 4 3 2 1

ISBN: 979-8-89188-118-1 (Hardcover)
ISBN: 979-8-89188-119-8 (eBook)

Library of Congress Control Number: 2024917207

Cover and layout design by Matthew Morse.

This publication is designed to provide accurate and authoritative information in regard to the subject matter covered. It is sold with the understanding that the publisher is not engaged in rendering legal, accounting, or other professional services. If legal advice or other expert assistance is required, the services of a competent professional person should be sought.

Advantage Books is an imprint of Advantage Media Group. Advantage Media helps busy entrepreneurs, CEOs, and leaders write and publish a book to grow their business and become the authority in their field. Advantage authors comprise an exclusive community of industry professionals, idea-makers, and thought leaders. For more information go to **advantagemedia.com**.

For Anita

CONTENTS

ACKNOWLEDGMENTS

BY TAYLOR BECKER

I would like to express my deepest gratitude to Anita Volz Wien for her unwavering generosity, dedication of time, and partnership. Her intellectual companionship to Byron throughout his life and her guidance to me in the completion of this project have been invaluable.

To my family and loved ones, including my parents William and Julee, siblings Megan and Josh, and my loving grandparents, your love and support throughout the years have been the foundation of my success. To Ralph, thank you for your boundless encouragement.

A heartfelt thank you to Maria Mousios for her long and tireless dedication to Byron professionally over the years and for her ongoing and selfless support to me personally in finishing this book.

I am grateful to my former colleagues at Blackstone, including Joseph Zidle, Caitlin Walsh, and Anav Bagla, for their encouragement and support in various ways throughout the years.

Lastly, my thanks to the Advantage Media team for their editorial assistance in helping get the final manuscript into publishable form, including Nate Best, Elizabeth Brueggemann, Ezra Byer, Annie LaGreca, and the design, print, and distribution teams.

PREFACE

BY TAYLOR BECKER

This book is dedicated to the memory and incredible life of Byron Wien, who passed away peacefully on October 25, 2023, at the age of ninety. Byron was a famed investor, with some going so far as to call him the "Oracle of Wall Street." He was my colleague of six years at Blackstone, where I had the great fortune to do investment strategy with him in his final act. He was my mentor and treasured friend.

Byron and I began writing this memoir in the summer of 2020, following the onset of the global pandemic. He was well known for his witticisms and incredible anecdotes, which he would recount with gusto at the dinner table or in a meeting. Many attempted to convince Byron to write these stories, but all failed. "The world already has enough books," he would say dismissively.

But I disagreed. So in that awful summer of 2020, when we were all isolated in our homes and learning to adjust to our new reality, I finally convinced Byron to spend one hour a week with me over Zoom to talk about his life. I was careful not to say, or even imply, that we were writing a book. Byron would grumble about being unable to go into the office or meet with clients face-to-face. He hated being stuck at home and wanted to get back in the game.

I saw my opportunity and struck. "Now that you have more free time, can't you spare an hour for me once a week?" He consented, so we started—an hour here and an hour there, and before either of us knew it, I had written tens of thousands of words over a matter of months. I sent this rough compilation to him somewhat smugly, and he was surprised to see the beginnings of this book. The best part was it was fascinating! I had him trapped. We were doing this, and from then on, we set out in earnest to craft this narrative.

I am grateful to have had this close-up opportunity to learn from Byron through coauthoring this memoir and our everyday interactions in our work together. There are three lessons in particular I have learned—and continue to learn—from this incredible man and his quintessentially American story.

LESSON 1: CURIOSITY

Byron never stopped learning. It was critical for his job, that strange vocation of "investment strategy," which requires boiling the ocean of anything that could be relevant to develop a view of the macroeconomic environment (in other words, everything). He would consume research reports, read thought-provoking books, and analyze papers on everything from semiconductors to blockchain to ChatGPT. Yes, it was necessary for his work. But he also had an insatiable love of learning for its own sake, even (and especially) when it challenged his preformed views.

That was one of the things I admired most about Byron. When I first met him, he was already entering the second half of his ninth decade of life, yet he never dismissed something because it was new-fangled or overhyped. A completely novel concept would emerge, like generative AI, and he would immediately begin trying to understand what it was, what it did, and what it meant for the world. In many ways, he made *me* feel like the curmudgeon. He was perpetually open to new information and constantly willing to accept facts that would change his opinions and refine his outlook.

This curiosity had a profound influence on my own life. When I started on his team as a young analyst, he would listen to my ideas and encourage me to push back on the views of people far senior to me. He took me seriously despite my lack of gray hairs, and that's a rare thing in the world, let alone in the staid, hierarchical realm of finance. When I had a good idea, he recognized it and nurtured it.

Fitzgerald once noted that the hallmark of first-rate intelligence is the capacity to juggle conflicting ideas while maintaining functionality. In that spirit, when we crafted our annual "Ten Surprises" list, Byron was open to entertaining all perspectives—no matter how contradictory they were to each other—as long as they defied conventional wisdom and could be backed up with evidence and sound reasoning.

The love of acquiring new knowledge and the intellectual flexibility to let that knowledge change one's preconceived notions are remarkable in any person. It's especially so in someone who has attained the distinction of having lived more than ninety years.

LESSON 2: GRIT

In her best-selling book *Grit*, Angela Duckworth argues that passion and perseverance, rather than natural talent, are the keys to success.[1] Byron was gritty in obvious ways, having accomplished so much in his life despite being orphaned in his teenage years. He also showed

---

1   Angela Duckworth, *Grit: The Power of Passion and Perseverance* (New York: Simon & Schuster, 2016).

obvious persistence in his dogged determination to continue working until the very end.

But Byron was gritty in other, more subtle ways. He often told the story of how his boss told him that things weren't working out when he started as an analyst on Wall Street. Byron was smart and worked hard, but he didn't seem to have an intuitive knack for finance. Rather than taking that as a sign he should pivot, he doubled down. He told his boss he was confident he could quickly turn things around. While Byron admitted later that this was a bit of a bluff, turn things around he did. He pushed through the failures and devoted himself to becoming a success.

Byron said he didn't do this by studying other successful people and trying to emulate them and beat them at their own game. He didn't try to be *better* than others; he tried to be *different*. One avenue he pursued as a portfolio analyst was the use of technical analysis (the use of price and volume data, usually displayed graphically) to gain an edge. At the time, the method was relatively unknown and viewed derisively by many as a means of analyzing financial markets. He didn't make his career as a technician, but he used it as one way to be different from others, and it worked. Byron turned things around through his perseverance and eventually rose the ranks to become a portfolio manager.

The other element of grit is passion. I mentioned Byron's passion for learning earlier, but he also had a zeal for his craft. Why did he continue working until the very end? He said it was because he loved his job so much that he would be doing it even if he weren't paid. He would be sitting in front of his Bloomberg Terminal, reading reports, listening to webinars, and speaking to various subject matter experts, regardless of the accolades or incentives involved. That's the kind of passion that defines grit and leads to success.

LESSON 3: HUMILITY

Finally, at the end of his storied career, Byron was eminently humble. In his words, "Younger people are naturally insecure and tend to overplay their accomplishments. Most people don't become comfortable with who they are until they're in their forties. By that time, they can underplay their achievements and become a nicer, more likable person. Try to get to that point as soon as you can."

Humility seems to be one of those things that can be inversely correlated with one's age and level of success. Most people start out relatively unknown and unsuccessful and feel the need to puff themselves up to convince others they are worth believing and investing in. Then, as time goes on and one's accolades become evident, a person can begin to let their achievements speak for themselves.

I can't speak to whether Byron was humble in his forties, but I can say that by the time he entered his ninth decade, when he had achieved more than ever, he was remarkably so. One of the most impactful things he ever told me was that he still struggled with imposter syndrome. Imagine that. He was one of the pioneers of the "investment strategist" profession. He had been chief strategist at Morgan Stanley and Blackstone. His opinions were sought after by Federal Reserve chairs, investing giants, business tycoons, politicians, academics, journalists, and more. He was right more often than not. Yet he still felt imposter syndrome. How freeing it was for me to have a mentor like this.

I believe this book is the perfect instruction manual for anyone who wants to be grittier, more curious, humbler, and generally more prepared to take the sorts of risks that set one up for an impactful life.

While the prologue is in my voice, recounting my journey with Byron Wien and the genesis of our project, the following pages are all in his words. As you read on, you'll experience the wisdom and anecdotes of a man whose career spanned decades, told through his own words. Byron's reflections are filled with the same enthusiasm and depth that he brought to his conversations, guiding you through the world of investment strategy with a mix of humor and sharp analysis. If it feels like he's speaking directly to you, that's because he often did just that—engaging his audience with a personal touch that made even complex ideas accessible.

BYRON'S THREE BIG RISKS

Risk is an important aspect of a successful life.

I took three major career risks, the first of which was attending Harvard College. While most people would consider this decision a no-brainer after I'd been accepted, for me, it felt like a big risk. Harvard was a thousand miles away from my home in Chicago. Most of my friends were attending the  University of Illinois, and this meant I would be going to Cambridge with no prearranged associations. It was also an incredibly competitive place, and I had no way of knowing whether I would succeed.

Thankfully, I took the risk, and it was at Harvard I learned how to think critically and turn my thoughts into words. These turned out to be two of the most important skills I would need later in my career. The second risk I took was moving to New York City. I had

1

always been fascinated by New York, primarily because of my interest in the theater, and the city had myriad productions both on and off Broadway at any given time.

When faced with that decision, I was working for a firm in Chicago after graduating from Harvard Business School (HBS). That firm acquired a New York–based restaurant and food service business, the Brass Rail, which had won the contract to provide concessions at the 1964–1965 New York World's Fair. The company needed to send a representative to supervise these New York–based activities, and they approached me to discuss the position. I jumped at the opportunity. I had never lived in New York, but I had always wanted to.

I sensed there were more smart people congregated there than anywhere else in the world. While I had plenty of smart friends in Chicago, I thought life in New York would be endlessly stimulating. And even though my first couple of years with the food service company did not lead anywhere in terms of my career, when that was over and I was supposed to move back to Chicago, I elected not to do so and tried to find a job in New York.

In hindsight, the move to New York City was a gamble that paid off. Despite my initial uncertainties and limited career prospects, the allure of the city's vibrant culture and the opportunity to connect with its brightest minds outweighed any doubts. Choosing to stay in New York was a nod to its unique potential for personal and professional development. This demonstrates that while certain decisions may seem risky or unconventional at first, embracing them can unlock doors to unanticipated opportunities and learning experiences, solidifying the idea that the pursuit of one's passions, even amid uncertainty, often yields substantial personal and professional growth.

The next big risk I took was to go to work at Morgan Stanley. I had been working as a security analyst and portfolio manager at a series of money management firms in New York, and I had achieved a reasonable amount of success doing it. However, I felt these jobs were confining. While I traveled all over the United States and occasionally to Europe, I wanted to travel more broadly. I also had never operated on a large platform, which I sensed would be important for me to achieve broader success. When Morgan Stanley approached me about becoming its first-ever US investment strategist, I felt there were many attractive elements. It would give me the opportunity to write, which was important to me, while contributing to the firm's business. It would also enable me to travel all over the world. It was exactly the job I thought would fulfill all my ambitions. But I had never been a strategist before, although I had done strategy work at various firms.

It was a big risk and one that was not lost on Morgan Stanley. The firm had originally offered me a partnership but eventually reneged, saying they would withhold that opportunity until I proved myself on the job. I took the job anyway and became successful, and it changed my life. Ultimately, embracing the unfamiliarity of the strategist role at Morgan Stanley taught me the value of stepping outside my comfort zone.

These examples illustrate the transformative power of embracing opportunities that challenge our existing boundaries, affirming that venturing into uncharted professional territories, despite apparent risks and initial setbacks, can lead to unprecedented growth and satisfaction.

Through my own life and the lives of others, I have learned that putting oneself at risk and staying at risk is the primary determinant of success. If you stay at risk, you will be challenged because you are willing to lose something. It's scary but exciting, and it will keep you getting up day after day.

Once you have achieved a lot in life, it's tempting to say "That's enough," or "Time to sit back and enjoy myself now." For me, there's never been such a thing as "enough." No matter how much I've achieved or done, I've always felt there was more to do. Part of that is because when you find a perfect job, whatever it might be, you don't want to quit, even if you could. It would have been easy for me not to be this way, given my background.

Because I was orphaned as a teenager and grew up nearly penniless, no one ever expected me to achieve much of anything. Achieving a moderate amount of success would have given me permission to hang my hat on a career. But that's not the way I'm wired. In this book, I hope to share my keys to staying at risk in one's life and, along the way, teach you a little bit about how the world, and the investing world in particular, has changed in the nine decades I've been on this earth. Here's to hoping the next nine decades are just as eventful.

Staying at risk has been one of the defining features of my life and career. It was the key to success. The last of my life lessons, "Never retire," is a related theme. By continuing to put yourself at risk in some way, you will continue to evolve. Never stop doing that. You stop living the day that you stop putting yourself at risk.

CHAPTER 1

FIND YOUR BIG IDEA

To be truly successful, you must do something big.

Even though I had been working since I was fifteen, it wasn't until I was fifty that I realized this. Whether observing my peers from my Harvard days or seeing the massive success the early hedge fund titans achieved, I recognized I had unfulfilled ambitions. I had always had good jobs and earned enough to live a comfortable life and pay all my expenses, but I had not built any significant wealth. I had enjoyed a stable and satisfying career, but it had been unspectacular.

So when I went to work at Morgan Stanley as their US investment strategist, I had a blank slate in front of me. I was the first person to hold this position, and the opportunities were endless. All I needed was a big idea. As a US strategist, I found my primary responsibility was dissecting and understanding the myriad factors influencing the US financial markets.

This task had me deeply entrenched in analyzing past events and trends. However, I found myself contemplating a more forward-looking approach. What if I ventured into speculating about future market movements instead of solely analyzing the past? This was undoubtedly a risk, as the future was inherently unpredictable.

Yet history and experience taught me that significant achievements often result from calculated risk-taking. Could stepping into the realm of informed speculation, armed with a deep understanding of market dynamics, be my pathway to success? While risky, this approach beckoned as a pathway not just to predict market trends but also to shape them, challenging the conventional boundaries of my role in pursuing something truly impactful.

My big idea was to develop "Ten Surprises" for the new year, to be announced in the first week of January. The definition of a "surprise" was an event the average investor would only give a one-out-of-three chance of taking place, but I thought of as probable to occur. I presented this idea to the firm, but they turned it down, saying I could get all of them wrong, which would humiliate me and, more importantly, embarrass Morgan Stanley. They didn't care much about my humiliation, they told me, but they cared a lot about their own embarrassment.

Nevertheless, I continued to advocate for this concept, and the firm eventually capitulated. The first edition of the Ten Surprises came out in 1986, and I have written them every year since at three different firms. The Ten Surprises became popular from the outset, and every year, I write an essay reviewing how I have done. We now have a team of people working on them, and we try hard to make them true surprises, not events likely to occur. Some are contrarian ideas, and some are in the direction of the consensus but simply more extreme. I've included a couple of early versions of the essay in the book's appendix.

Over the years, I have probably gotten an average of around 60 percent correct. Getting a high grade has never been the primary goal.

I only wanted to stretch the thinking of my colleagues and clients and push them to consider ideas or events that they don't think are all that likely to materialize. One of the Surprises that proved to be the biggest hit was in 2008 when Barack Obama was fourteen points behind Hillary Clinton in the Democratic primary polls. My Surprise that year claimed Obama would be nominated and go on to win the presidency.

For the past decade, I have taken a million dollars of my own money and put it in around eight investable surprises. That has proven to be a profitable strategy, sometimes even beating the market. Here, I bring it back to the concept of risk. The Ten Surprises was an initial risk I took to achieve great success.

I stay at personal risk in terms of my reputation each year when I put my name and those of my colleagues on the list. And I stay at financial risk when I put my money where my mouth is by investing capital in the ideas I claim are probable.

ORIGINS OF MY LIFE'S LESSONS

While the Ten Surprises required an active and imaginative approach to forecasting, the genesis of my "Life's Lessons" was an unexpected divergence from my routine analytical work, more a product of chance than intention.

At an annual conference hosted by my close friend Dick Strong amid discussions centered on market forecasts—interest rates, oil prices, Federal Reserve policies—Dick proposed a novel idea. He noticed the redundancy in the conference topics and saw potential for a refreshing change in me. Despite my initial protests of expertise confined to my professional realm, Dick encouraged me to share the broader lessons gleaned over a lifetime.

His insistence led to an impromptu presentation on the wisdom accumulated through personal experiences and reflections, a departure from the conference's core focus but one that resonated deeply with the audience. This serendipitous moment highlighted the value of diversifying dialogue in professional gatherings. It marked the beginning of what would become a cherished and personally significant collection of insights known as "Life's Lessons."

Following my impromptu sharing of twelve lessons at that conference, an unforeseen leak led to coverage by CNBC, setting off a chain of events that caught me off guard. By the time the article was published, I was with Blackstone, bound by an agreement that granted the firm first rights to any of my publications—a clause I had now inadvertently breached. The revelation prompted Pete Rose, Blackstone's head of public affairs, to warn me of my potential jeopardy.

"Your career is in danger," he told me. Fortunately, Pete had a solution. He suggested I officially document and expand upon these lessons under Blackstone's banner, a move designed to preempt unauthorized publication and assert the originality and ownership of my insights. I was encouraged to exceed the original dozen; this initiative was a corrective measure. It offered an opportunity to further refine and share the life lessons that had unexpectedly resonated with a wider audience.

So I wrote down Twenty Life Lessons, which appear below. This list could be understood as a summary of the most important lessons I've learned in ninety years, nearly two-thirds of which I have spent in the business world, particularly finance. The chapters that follow try to bring these lessons to life.

TWENTY LIFE LESSONS

1. Concentrate on finding a big idea that will impact the people you want to influence. If you want to be successful and live a long, stimulating life, keep yourself at risk intellectually all the time.

2. Network intensely. Luck plays a big role in life, and there is no better way to increase your luck than by knowing as many people as possible. Nurture your network by sending articles, books, and emails to people to show you're thinking about them. Write op-eds and thought pieces for major publications. Organize discussion groups to bring your thoughtful friends together.

3. When you meet someone new, treat that person as a friend. Assume he or she is a winner and will become a positive force in your life. Most people wait for others to prove their value. Give them the benefit of the doubt from the start. Occasionally, you will be disappointed, but your network will broaden rapidly if you follow this path.

4. Read all the time. Don't just do it because you're curious about something; read actively. Have a point of view before you start a book or article and see if what you think is confirmed or refuted by the author. If you do that, you will read faster and comprehend more.

5. Get enough sleep. Seven hours will do until you're sixty, eight from sixty to seventy, and nine thereafter—which might include eight hours at night and a one-hour afternoon nap.

6. Evolve. Try to think of your life in phases so you can avoid burnout. Do the number crunching in the early phase of your career. Try developing concepts later on. Stay at risk throughout the process.

7. Travel extensively. Try to get everywhere before you wear out. Attempt to meet local, interesting people where you travel and keep in contact with them throughout your life. See them when you return to a place.

8. When meeting someone new, try to discover what formative experience occurred in their lives before they were seventeen. I believe that some important event in everyone's youth influences everything that occurs afterward.

9. In philanthropy, I try to relieve pain rather than spread joy. Music, theater, and art museums have many affluent supporters, give the best parties, and can add to your social luster in a community. They don't need you. Social services, hospitals, and educational institutions can improve the world and help the disadvantaged reach the American dream.

10. Younger people are naturally insecure and tend to overplay their accomplishments. Most people don't become comfortable with who they are until they're in their forties. By then, they can underplay their achievements and become nicer, more likable people. Try to get to that point as soon as you can.

11. Take the time to pat those who work for you on the back when they do good work. Most people are so focused on the next challenge that they fail to thank those who support them. It is important to do this. It motivates and inspires people and encourages them to perform at a higher level.

12. When someone extends kindness to you, write them a handwritten note, not an email. Handwritten notes make an impact and are not quickly forgotten.

13. At the beginning of every year, think of ways to do your job better than you have ever done it. Write them down, and when the year is over, look at what you have set out for yourself.

14. The hard way is always the right way. Never take shortcuts, except when driving home from the Hamptons. Shortcuts can be construed as sloppiness, a career killer.

15. Don't try to be better than your competitors; try to be different. There will always be someone smarter than you, but there may not be someone more imaginative.

16. When seeking a career as you come out of school or making a job change, always take the job that looks like it will be the most enjoyable. If it pays the most, you're lucky. If it doesn't, take it anyway. I took a severe pay cut to take each of the two best jobs I've ever had, and they both turned out to be exceptionally rewarding financially.

17. There is a perfect job out there for everyone. Most people never find it. Keep looking. The goal of life is to be happy, and the right job is essential to that.

18. When your children are grown, or if you have no children, always find someone younger to mentor. It is very satisfying to help someone steer through life's obstacles, and you'll be surprised at how much you will learn in the process.

19. Every year, try doing something you have never done before that is totally out of your comfort zone. It could be running a marathon, attending a conference that interests you on an offbeat subject that will be populated by people very different from your usual circle of associates and friends, or traveling to an obscure destination alone. This will add to the essential process of self-discovery.

20. Never retire. If you work forever, you can live forever. I know there is abundant biological evidence against this theory, but I'm going with it anyway.

When I started writing the Ten Surprises, this was the first time anyone was doing something like this. I felt that it would generate a lot more interest than just writing about the market, the Fed, and oil prices every week. It became popular right away and became my signature product. When I planned to leave Morgan Stanley in 2005, the firm owned the Ten Surprises, and they had the service mark.

Not wishing for my Ten Surprises to meet an untimely end, I asked the firm if I could take the concept with me and continue to publish it. They replied in the affirmative, with the condition that I would have to license it from them. John Mack, the CEO, pretended to be very serious and gravely shook his head. He wasn't sure, he said, that I would be willing to pay the license fee. "Try me," I replied. "How much?" His response? "One dollar a year."

I'm known for being extremely frugal (arguably to a fault), but even I could cough up that much cash. And I've continued to do so. Now every year, on the second day after presenting the Ten Surprises at Blackstone, I go back to Morgan Stanley to present the Surprises to their sales force, and I give the one-dollar payment to the head of research at Morgan Stanley Investment Management.

FIND BIG IDEAS TO INVEST IN

Finding a big idea is critical for your career. But it's also important to understand if you want to be an investor, particularly if you want to invest in the stock market. Analysts will often look at a stock's expected earnings in the next quarter or watch for the next piece of government data that might impact that company.

If you want to be better than the rest, take a step back and analyze investment opportunities with the paradigm of the "big idea." Does the company have one? Examine each firm's products and services.

Have they hit on something that people will want for a long time? Is that company regenerating its offerings on a continuous basis?

While I will discuss my investment philosophy in greater detail later in this book, the context of embracing big ideas and the willingness to take risks bear a brief discussion in this section. Identifying companies that have not only discovered their big idea but also possess the acumen to capitalize on it is foundational to my strategy. These selections, often growth stocks, are the linchpins of long-term holding strategies. Reflecting on my tenure as a portfolio manager, I find it evident that the bulk of my most successful investments were precisely in such stocks.

The advantage of the equity market is its potential for outsize returns when one invests early in companies poised for significant growth. This journey, however, is fraught with the risk of total loss, a reality I've encountered through investments in both individual stocks and hedge funds. Yet it is this very risk that paves the way for remarkable gains, as evidenced by my investments in the technology and biotech sectors, yielding returns many times over the initial stake.

My method for uncovering exceptional stocks throughout my career hinged on finding companies with underappreciated yet promising products backed by robust research and development efforts. This approach is predicated on the belief in investing not merely in a singular product or idea but in the continual innovation that drives a company's growth.

This investment ethos has been instrumental in my journey from modest beginnings to achieving a sizable net worth today. Starting with an initial capital of $50,000, I could never have envisioned the scale of success that would come, particularly in the 1970s when my account ballooned to ten times its size, a fortune in my eyes at the time.

At any moment, the market harbors only a handful of true, sustainable growth stocks characterized by innovative products and the capability to rejuvenate their product lines. Recognizing these companies is crucial, as they represent the "ten-baggers" that can significantly augment a portfolio. My experiences with early investments in companies like Intel, Biogen, and FedEx, and more recent giants such as Meta, Amazon, and Google, illustrate the dynamic nature of growth stocks and the necessity to move on as they mature.

The landscape of growth stocks is in constant flux, demanding discernment in timing entry and exit points. Forecasts by leading technology experts suggest the emergence of a new cadre of tech behemoths within the next decade, akin to today's FAANG stocks, with Microsoft added for a comprehensive perspective. Identifying and investing in these future leaders early on is a pivotal opportunity for today's growth investors.

So we've discussed the importance of "big ideas" in your life and the companies you invest in. Now let's add another lesson to this first one, which is closely related.

DON'T TRY TO BE BETTER; TRY TO BE DIFFERENT

Don't try to be better than your competitors; try to be different.

> There will always be someone smarter than you, but there may not be someone more imaginative.

I am pretty smart, but I've never considered myself the smartest in the room, let alone in the vaunted classrooms of Harvard College or Harvard Business School. What I have always considered myself to be, however, is creative. Whether in writing poetry or reviewing theater, both of which I did at Harvard College, I have always found a way to put my own unique spin on things.

Wall Street is full of terrifically clever, intelligent people. It's nearly impossible to be the smartest in a boardroom at 345 Park Avenue (Blackstone's headquarters) or any other boardroom on Wall Street or Midtown Manhattan, for that matter. But folks in any industry, any company, any team, can be subject to "groupthink"—that tricky thing where people, whether in a perfectly understandable desire for comity (or a less-acceptable desire to avoid conflict at all costs), do not practice creativity and strive for intellectual diversity. That's one thing I'll never be able to stomach.

So I was pretty smart but very creative. When I was ready to start my career, I contacted successful people from my HBS graduating class to see if they knew of a job for me. One of my fellow alums had started a small money management firm: Brokaw, Schaenen and Clancy. Brokaw and Schaenen had been investment bankers at Dillon Reed.

Brokaw came from a wealthy New York family, and Schaenen's father was head of Smith Barney. Clancy had gone to HBS and was an institutional stockbroker at Smith Barney who traded for Brokaw and Schaenen. They started a firm with their three names, which became very successful. Bill Brokaw remembered me as a smart kid from HBS and offered me a job as a security analyst, thus beginning my introduction to the investment business in 1965.

When Bill Brokaw originally hired me at Brokaw, Schaenen and Clancy, he thought I would be a terrific security analyst, given my experience working in corporations like Foote Cone and Armour Research. Unfortunately, at the end of the year, he came into my office and said, "This isn't working out. You haven't really contributed. Maybe this isn't the right place for you. We think you should look for another job."

Here I was, thirty years old, with two Harvard degrees, and I was going to be out on the street. Bill said that there were other firms that were impressed with me, and he could set up some interviews. I didn't want to do that, though, as I had only been at the firm for a year.

I told him, "Bill, I think I'm on the brink of turning this around. If you just give me a little more time, I think I can begin to contribute." (I had absolutely no basis for making this statement.) He didn't buy it, but he indicated they wouldn't push me out the door yet. They would transition me over time because the firm was getting a lot of new business and needed help getting the work done. This was my window of opportunity to turn things around, and I jumped at the chance. I clearly wasn't getting the job done just by doing what I had been taught, so I needed to do something different to prove myself and add value in a differentiated way.

To start, I doubled down on my effort. I might not have been the most naturally talented analyst there, so I set out to be the hardest working. I got into the office at seven every morning and was there until eleven every night. Eventually, despite Bill's skepticism—or perhaps because of it—I began to positively impact the portfolio's performance. And within a year, I was made a firm partner.

How did I turn it around so quickly? One factor in my success was that I had developed a skill that didn't previously exist at the firm. At that time, technical analysis—the analysis of stock price movements and the patterns they created—was very controversial. Merrill Lynch had a famous technician, Bob Farrell, a contemporary of mine, and other firms had technicians too, yet the practice was never widely respected. I thought there might be something to it, so I explored it as much as possible.

A speech at the New York Society of Security Analysts featured a presentation from well-known investor Sam Steadman, an early hedge fund manager. Steadman got up and supported his investment ideas with a series of charts. During the question-and-answer period, someone raised his hand and said, "This is the worst meeting I've ever been to. I came here to listen to someone who was supposedly one of the great investors of our time, and he turns out to be just another goddamned chartist." (This was the most derisive word one could use about a technician in those days.)

Steadman replied, to his credit, "Well, I see you know all about me. Did you know I'm also a hunter?" The audience member replied that he didn't. Steadman continued, "Well, when I go hunting, I bring my gun along, and I also bring my dog, but I don't give him the gun."

Despite the derision technical analysis received from many, I was convinced it could be a valuable tool. At that time, a group of technicians met weekly in the Wall Street area. I applied for admission to that group and was accepted. Every week, I would go and listen, and I read several books by James Granville and others who practiced technical analysis. I brought the concept to Brokaw and used it to help them pick stocks, and it worked. It was a key reason I turned my career around and made partner. Some of the great investors of our time, such as Stan Druckenmiller and Paul Tudor Jones, pay a lot of attention to technical analysis. It's another tool that one can use to improve one's investment performance.

BEING DIFFERENT IS NOT WITHOUT DANGER

Being different comes with risks of its own, of course. In 1996, I received a call from the Federal Reserve inviting me to come down to Washington to present. Federal Reserve Chairman Alan Greenspan was convening a meeting that would include his Fed board colleagues and a panel of nine market experts, including myself. My fellow participants included Abby Cohen, then the chief equity strategist for Goldman Sachs, and Robert Schiller, a renowned Yale University economist, among others. While those of us in the room were asked not to divulge the contents of that meeting, I can share my views at that time.

We were each to speak alphabetically, and when it was my turn, Greenspan asked me, "Wien, I understand you're bullish. Why?"

I had my beloved dividend discount model with me—which I still use today—and I passed out copies to the key decision-makers at the meeting. The dividend discount model, which relates equity earnings to the level of the ten-year Treasury yield, showed that the market's price in 1996 was fairly priced, or at least not overvalued. That view turned out to be quite different from Greenspan's, though I didn't know it at the time.

The Fed Chair responded by saying that he believed the market was forming a bubble. I retorted with the data from my model, and a discussion ensued. After the meeting at the Federal Reserve, I called New York and spoke to the heads of fixed-income trading and equity trading at Morgan Stanley. I relayed to them that I had testified before the Federal Reserve and believed I had convinced Alan Greenspan that the market was not overvalued. That evening in 1996, unbeknownst to me, Greenspan went to the Mayflower Hotel and gave his famous "Irrational Exuberance" speech.

I left Washington to go to Houston for client meetings and was asleep in my hotel room when I got a phone call from the head of fixed-income trading. It started with the term "You idiot" and proceeded from there (the rest of which I cannot quote in a family-friendly publication). However, the gist of his message to me was that I had misinterpreted Greenspan's reaction to my presentation and that markets were going down.

Shortly after that, I received a call from the head of equity trading with the same message. So this was a case where I had gone to Washington to plead the bullish case, and Greenspan didn't buy it at all, as his speech to the contrary showed. The markets reacted quite negatively to this entire episode. My vindication was forthcoming, however, and I eventually proved to be right in my bullishness, as the market continued to go up after it recovered from the Irrational Exuberance dip, and it didn't peak until 1999.

The lessons I learned from this episode were twofold: First, be careful not to overstate your confidence level when you think you have convinced someone of something. I would not have caught as much flak from my colleagues at Morgan Stanley if I had simply relayed what took place in that meeting. The second lesson, however, is that I am glad I stuck to my guns and did not capitulate on my bullishness the moment the markets took a dip. My view turned out to be right in the long run, and I was glad to have been willing to take a differentiated view.

Whatever your vocation or situation,
you can turn it around if you find a creative way
to be different from everyone else.

You may never be the most naturally talented or intelligent, but you can be the one who spends the time to come up with a big idea that no one else has considered or shares an idiosyncratic perspective that someone with only your diverse, unique background and experiences would think up.

This last point is important. You may come from a difficult background like I did. Recognize that while this may have set you back in certain ways, it's part of you. So own it. It's up to you to celebrate who you are. Don't expect other people to do it for you.

If you feel that your talent and desire for hard work are not being sufficiently utilized, it's up to you to press your superiors to use you more effectively, and you must be aggressive in doing it, even if it proves to be an irritant to your managers. It's up to you to forge your own future. Nobody else will do it for you. Doing this will set you apart and help you to be different from your competitors.

CHAPTER 2

EVOLVE EACH YEAR

Evolve. Try to think of your life in phases so you can avoid burnout. Do the number crunching in the early phase of your career. Try developing concepts later on. Stay at risk throughout the process.

It is critical to avoid complacency in every phase of your life.

If you are successful in your career, you will probably move through various phases. You might start out as a junior employee, do great work, get recognized, be promoted, and so on. You may even reach the top of your respective ladder. Perhaps you start your own company, grow it, and eventually reach the point where you can monetize your share. No matter your path, there will be various chances to move up or move out. It's critical, no matter where you are or what you are doing, that you continue to evolve by keeping yourself personally at risk throughout the process.

Complacency can sneak up on you. There is often a natural, steep learning curve whenever you start something new. As you hone your craft, you will find that the learning curve flattens out. That's not necessarily a bad thing, but you must be careful that you never stop learning or that your learning pace does not decrease substantially. If that happens, you may leave some of your skills or ambitions on the table.

Another danger is becoming too comfortable. The more senior you get, the more ownership in a company you begin to take, and the more indispensable you might become (or at least you might feel that way). Never let yourself feel indispensable. No one is. More importantly, if you let yourself feel too secure, you will stop taking the necessary risks to continue your personal and career progressions.

Always seek new ways to stretch your ability. This will benefit you personally and professionally and help you fend off contentment without progress. Engaging in critical self-analysis and soliciting feedback from others are other ways to ensure continual growth. This can be done informally with your friends, mentors, and colleagues, but it can also be instituted formally at the organizational level.

At Blackstone, we conduct a 360-degree review process each year. This process involves selecting a group of up to fifteen individuals, including peers and senior and junior colleagues, to provide comments on our performance. In addition, we are required to write an appraisal for ourselves. This process is highly beneficial, as it allows me to analyze my performance at a high level and set goals for the year ahead. I write an appraisal every year and believe it pays off for me.

Another reason to keep evolving is to avoid burnout. I've encountered this as one of the biggest problems for people in the financial services business. Still, it's a prevalent issue in all industries in various ways and to different degrees. The way to prevent this issue is to do different things throughout your career. For example, I started in advertising, went into management consulting, worked in a corporate role at a company, and became a security analyst and then a portfolio manager. I became an equity sector strategist and ultimately landed as a global equity strategist, both on the sell and buy sides. By doing these different things, I kept from burning out. I also replaced myself twice. The first time was in 2001, when we hired Steve Galbraith to succeed me as chief US investment strategist at Morgan Stanley. The second was in 2018, when we found Joe Zidle to replace me as chief investment strategist at Blackstone.

By periodically replacing yourself, you can remain adaptable and stay ahead of the game. It ensures that you stay calm in one role, allowing fresh perspectives to enter and helping you pursue new challenges, which is essential for ongoing growth and avoiding stagnation. Even now, I have evolved into the "senior strategist" role, where I can work on various things but not dig as deeply into them as I once did.

Every industry changes because institutions consist of people who constantly cycle in and out and make their own decisions. Economies change too; new technologies are invented, and market structures are constantly in flux. When the world changes around you, what do you do? You need to evolve with it. That's what I've done, and it's kept me going in my ninth decade.

THE EVOLUTION OF MONEY MANAGEMENT

When I started in the money management industry in 1965, more than a half century ago, it was a simpler time to be a security analyst. One did not necessarily need to view the world with a wide lens to perform well. I, for example, didn't know what interest rate levels were in various parts of the world. I didn't know how the dollar traded against the lira, franc, or pound. I thought the US stock market was almost entirely dependent on the performance of the US economy, and I paid no attention to the influence of foreign economies on US exports.

It was easier to be narrow-minded and still be a good security analyst of US stocks. That has changed as the world economy has become more interconnected than ever, and larger shares of the revenues of American firms are derived from foreign markets. The markets have also grown more complex over time, with the proliferation of new financial instruments and even industries that no one would have learned about at HBS in the 1950s. In 1965, Mike Milken had yet to invent junk bonds. Leveraged buyouts were few and far between. There was basically no derivatives business and only a few hedge funds.

The industry underwent a rapid transformation in the 1980s. In 1982, the Federal Reserve became accommodative, partially responding to the Mexican financial crisis. As a result, the stock market took off. This coincided with the yield on equities dropping below that of bonds. A primary reason for this was the evolution of how companies thought about using the capital on their balance sheets. Business managers recognized that paying dividends wasn't always the best use of a company's cash. Growth companies, for example, could derive a greater return from investing in the business than they would from paying dividends to shareholders. As a result, the traditional fashion of maintaining a dividend payout ratio of 40 percent ended, and the concept of growth companies reinvesting cash in their business—rather than paying it out in dividends—began.

By 1982, the excitement of Polaroid, Xerox, and Control Data Corporation had worn off, but a whole new generation of growth stocks was born. By the 1990s, the internet had been formed, and stocks like Amazon and Google began to gather attention. We have been in a growth stock environment ever since. There were setbacks, notably in the bear market, that resulted from the global financial crisis. However, that was caused by the bubble in housing, as opposed to any fundamental reversal in the fortune of growth stocks, and growth stocks have generally continued to lead to this day.

There are fewer stocks in which people can invest today, with the number of listed companies falling precipitously over the past few decades. There are fewer listed companies today than in 1976, despite gross domestic product being more than three times as large, and the stock market capitalization being many multiples greater. One reason is that young companies can raise money privately without going public. That allows the founders of a business to build up their stake in the company without diluting their interests as seriously as they would with an initial public offering. This is particularly so for early start-up companies, which many consider to be the growth companies of tomorrow.

The ability to raise private capital is good for companies with able entrepreneurs but bad for companies where outside professional management helps shepherd a company to the next level. Mark Zuckerberg can lead Facebook to be a major company in social media and technology, but only some founders of an internet-related firm have that skill. This requires much caution for investors who wish to invest in growth stocks.

Asset allocation has also changed. The traditional model portfolio typically comprised 60 percent equities and 40 percent fixed income. It has evolved, and in recent years, a model portfolio has generally been closer to 70 percent equities and 30 percent fixed income, not least of which because of historically low yields in the bond markets over the last decade.

That was before the advent of alternative asset classes. Over the past few years, I have recommended 30 percent in alternatives—10 percent in private equity, 10 percent in hedge funds, and 10 percent in alternative credit. I've never been a big fan of investing in commodities as a stable portfolio allocation. In recent years, I have generally hesitated to recommend investing in Treasury bonds because I don't think the yield is sufficient. The private real estate asset class has proven to be an interesting alternative to traditional fixed-income investments, as it tends to provide adequate returns with limited risk and illiquidity.

There has also been a significant change in the compensation of people who work in finance. When I began working in finance in 1965, I made $20,000 a year, similar to what a doctor or lawyer might have generally made. Over the next two decades, earnings for the medical, legal, and financial professions grew in parallel. However, after 1982, compensation in finance became much more generous.

Firms were making much more money and paid their key employees accordingly. Only a few people made over $1 million annually in 1981. By the end of the 1980s, that was not an uncommon figure for people on Wall Street to be earning. People who could suddenly navigate the newfound complexity of the markets by specializing in derivatives, options, leveraged buyouts, and junk bonds could create enormous profits for their firms and themselves.

And the financial markets continue to evolve. Today, cryptocurrencies are another new financial instrument that has been developed and introduced to markets, enriching a new generation of entrepreneurs and investors with the technical expertise and risk tolerance to profit from them. Much skepticism surrounds these instruments, as people were cautious about those novel developments in the 1980s. There are prominent investors like John Paulsen, who made a lot of money shorting subprime mortgages and who feel that cryptocurrencies have no intrinsic value, whereas other investors are true believers.

I remain skeptical of these new currencies. I accept that cryptocurrencies are good trading vehicles, but holding them in a portfolio as a store of value or hedge against volatility does not make sense because they have inherent volatility. I have a better understanding of the role of gold in this regard, which fluctuates within narrow limits and does provide some protection against equity market volatility.

The most significant change I have witnessed over the past half century relates to the change in views on interest rates, which have been in a secular bull market for most of my time in the business. When I began my career, there were several prominent strategists, such as Lucien O. Hooper and Gerald Loeb. These venerable figures on Wall Street walked down the street in three-piece suits, and the crowds parted before them.

The strategists of that era generally believed in a specific principle about interest rates: the yield on stocks should always be higher than on bonds. After all, stocks are risky assets, and (so the theory went) they should pay a higher return than that which you could get on a safe asset like a government Treasury bond.

For my first seventeen years in the industry, the Standard & Poor's 500 and the Dow Jones Industrial Average did not make significant gains. One could make money in the market by investing in growth stocks, such as the "Nifty Fifty," which rose to astronomical prices before 1970. But it was a tough place to make money. By the 1980s, as I mentioned before, the stocks' yield dropped below the bonds' yield, and the greatest bull market of all time began. Many of the leading strategists at the time turned bearish, and as a result, they missed out on the bull market that ran from 1982 to 1999.

This highlights the importance of intellectual humility and flexibility in investing in a business. Even the most sturdy-seeming theories can fail when a catalyst changes the relationship that certain variables have with one another. One should always be willing to adjust one's views and portfolios accordingly when the facts change.

In short, the transformation of the industry that I have described shows the increasing complexity of the market and the necessity for analysts and investors to deepen their skills and understanding of a broad range of products to succeed. Even if someone does not specialize in these areas, they do have to understand the interplay between them. For example, if someone did not understand the significance of subprime mortgage derivatives, they could not have understood, let alone anticipated, what was unfolding in the 2007–2008 housing debacle in the United States.

Following the COVID-19 pandemic, the market has been supported by nearly unprecedented amounts of fiscal and monetary stimulus. On the fiscal side, the United States is running enormous budget deficits and has increased the federal debt-to-GDP ratio from 30 percent in 2000 to 70 percent in 2015 to over 100 percent of the GDP today. The Fed's balance sheet went from $1 trillion in 2007 to $8 trillion (and counting) now. Unless you are a die-hard modern monetary theorist, you should be worried that this trend is not sustainable and will lead to a bad outcome. Nobody knows when this will happen. But in the meantime, markets have continued to make new highs as recently as 2022, while calamities occur around the world and geopolitical tensions bubble. This is what happens when we experiment with unprecedented liquidity, as we have done over the past decade.

The question is, What does this all mean, and how will it end? The bears think the liquidity and fiscal spending have been excessive and must end badly. The bulls feel that growth stocks are the place to be and that while the government will eventually reduce its accommodation, large budget deficits are here to stay, and we will never run a budget surplus again. These issues will be resolved over the next decade. When the history books are written about the next half century, the resolution of this issue will be among the most impactful for the economy and financial services industry.

ADVICE FOR YOUNG PEOPLE

I think a lot about the future. My great-nephews and great-nieces all have children, and I think about what the world will be like for those kids. When I was growing up, it was a simpler time. Most kids went to public schools and state universities. They majored in some field that would help them get a good job and proceeded to work long careers for a single company or a family business.

Today, it seems much different. Most of the young people I know in New York attend private schools. They try to get into Ivy League colleges, and many have to go to "backup" schools. They use connections to get jobs and face a world of uncertainty. They worry about things like the war in Ukraine and what that will do to geopolitical stability. They worry about the US relationship with China and what it means for supply chains. They worry about inflation and earning enough money to buy a home without parental support.

For many young people today, the future seems filled with risk— not the good kind I've been talking about that allows you to challenge yourself and move forward. Young people today feel a sense of foreboding of the troubled, unknown future, filled with risk skewed more to the downside than the upside. Whereas when my generation was starting, we felt the future was filled with opportunity.

If you were born in the 1930s, the period after World War II was one of tremendous opportunity; it was easier to get into a good college because of the low birth rates during the Depression. Getting a good job was simpler because fewer people were entering the workforce, and it was easier to get promoted because the talent pool was smaller.

I benefited from all those things and have had a terrific life. That does not mean, of course, that I did not have some dark periods. I did. But I was never worried that I would be unemployed or hungry. I don't think it's the same for kids today. The competition is tougher, and the opportunities are more limited.

That said, I'd encourage you to approach the future optimistically. Stay informed about your challenges, but don't let them bring you down. Life is a matter of making the right choices, so choose to be an optimist. Although not everything will be within your control, success comes from making good decisions about the opportunities that come your way.

TRY NEW THINGS

Some of these important choices include the necessity of pushing yourself to try new things, and that is Life Lesson Nineteen:

> Every year, try doing something you have never done before that is totally out of your comfort zone. This expands you.

This can include doing athletic things, such as the years I spent ski racing. It might involve attending conferences where you associate with people different from your normal circle of friends. For example, I attend parties where I think the attendees will challenge me or stretch my thinking, and I've traveled to third-world countries alone. I think I've grown as a person as a result.

If I look back on my career, I see that I took several risks in building my future. I took a big risk moving to New York while working for Interstate United. I took another big risk entering the investment business when I had no training or experience in the field. Another was joining Morgan Stanley to be a strategist, a job I had never done before and in which I was expected to perform at a high level. But in each instance, I had the good judgment that when I was confronted with an attractive opportunity, I took it, regardless of the risk that came with it.

That's how someone needs to approach his or her career and life generally. You will be presented with opportunities, and some people are more secure with their current situation than the new job or change being presented to them. But if you think it's something you can do and that it could improve your life, you must be willing to leap. It's the only way to move forward. If you're faced with a new opportunity and you think it could be a big step forward, you must take it, regardless of the risk.

CHAPTER 3

NURTURE YOUR NETWORK

Network intensely. Luck plays a big role in life, and there is no better way to increase your luck than by knowing as many people as possible. Nurture your network by sending articles, books, and emails to people to show that you're thinking about them. Write op-eds and thought pieces for major publications. Organize discussion groups to bring your thoughtful friends together.

Knowing as many influential people as possible is a noble objective of anybody in any business.

Over the years, I have developed a broad network of influential people from various sources. Some are from my professional and social life: my contacts from when I worked at Morgan Stanley, people I have met through attending various conferences, and mates from tennis.

By having a broad network, you have somebody you can go to when you need to check out a person, a company, or an industry. This network can be very helpful in your career. Most importantly, it adds to the joy of your daily life. So make it part of your daily routine. Schedule meals with people, and get to know them socially. When you get an opportunity to join a group, professional or otherwise, take advantage of it. You may find that it does not suit you or is not useful, in which case you can drop out.

Relationships need to be nurtured, and it takes active effort. I cannot emphasize the importance of this lesson enough. Since my first one out of business school, all the jobs I have ever had have come through personal contacts. The more people you know, the more people you can seek out if you want to change jobs. They can make connections for you and help you make wise decisions.

One of the most important by-products of an active network is how much you can learn from these people. Every year, I organize a series of summer lunches and always get a lot out of them. This includes not only the substantive material that people present when they comment on the issues of the day but also from thinking about these individuals in relation to their careers: what they've built, what problems they've encountered, and how they've handled them.

One obvious but important way to expand your network is in professional settings. Weiss, Peck & Greer had several astute analysts, and the company prospered during the 1970s and early 1980s. It was during this period that I started attending a group that came to be known as the "Third Thursday" group. The nucleus of this group was composed of the directors of research at various firms. Arthur Zeikel from Merrill Lynch was one prominent member.

The Third Thursday group would meet monthly to discuss trends, investment ideas we liked, and the research we had been conducting. This group still convenes to this day, and I chair the December meeting where we discuss my annual list of Ten Surprises. Similar groups were initiated in those days, the most notable being the Enrichment Group and Concept Group. Various hedge fund managers started these and, as far as I know, continue to this day, primarily functioning as stock-picking groups.

I believe getting to know as many intelligent people as possible is essential, including in casual and social settings. When I began spending summers in the Hamptons in Eastern Long Island in 1970, that became clear to me. As mentioned before, one of the reasons I wanted to move to New York from Chicago was that in New York, I would encounter many highly intelligent people and learn from them. I have not been disappointed. Some of these people have homes in the Hamptons, and people are more relaxed out there. Interactions with them are informal, but no less productive than meeting in a conference room in the city.

About twenty years ago, I started to attend an annual July Fourth party given by Elizabeth "Lally" Graham Weymouth, the daughter of Katharine Graham, the late publisher of the *Washington Post*. Lally would invite about three hundred people to a Fourth of July dinner, including prominent people in the Hamptons and politicians like Chuck Schumer, Rudy Giuliani, and others. I knew many of the people at these celebrations, and I had one- or two-minute interludes with each of them. This helped solidify some new friendships, which, in turn, helped build up attendance at my own Benchmark Lunches.

THE BENCHMARK LUNCHES

One of my favorite things is organizing a series of luncheons in the Hamptons on four successive Fridays each summer. We have many notable participants, and I do get some luminaries in attendance. I invite about 140 people, and about 100 attend four meetings with roughly 20 to 30 in each meeting. The meetings are substantive, and I organize an agenda and moderate each one. People network to some degree, but that is not the main purpose. People can convene early and say hello to each other, but by the time the meeting starts promptly at 1:15 p.m., it continues without interruption until 3:00 p.m., and side conversations are not permitted.

The lunches originated nearly forty years ago. Around the inception of the Ten Surprises, Charles Phillips, a managing director at Morgan Stanley, invited me to lunch at Jack Nash's house at Water Mill. We talked about the outlook for the world in the coming year. The next year, I suggested inviting someone else and kept making suggestions. When the group's size reached fourteen people, Jack said his chef could not handle any more.

By then, my wife Anita and I had moved to a bigger house, and I could hold a similar lunch on a different Friday. So I did that, and invited fourteen more people, bringing our total group size to twenty-eight between the two lunches. I kept inviting people and increasing the size, eventually expanding to a third and finally a fourth lunch. I've continued these lunches to this day, and in 2020, we reached a record five lunches, as they were all virtual due to the COVID-19 pandemic.

The lunches include many serious investors, including leaders of financial services firms, hedge fund and real estate investors, academics, and people in the policy world. Most people reside in eastern Long Island, but others make the trip out just for the lunch. I learn a lot from these interactions, and they provide a great foundation for the Ten Surprises, helping me understand what the consensus believes will happen in the coming months and years.

By distilling the contents of four two-hour lunches, I can create a high-level summary of the views and expectations of some of the smartest people around. That's a sufficient basis for me to consider how the future might deviate from that. The Benchmark Lunches are also useful for suggesting categories for the Ten Surprises. With that as a basis, it is incumbent on me to come up with specific ideas within those areas.

Why do people come to a serious meeting like this during the summer on what is typically a beautiful Friday afternoon? To some extent, it's to be in the presence of the impressive people who show up. They want to hear what some of the smartest investors of our time have to say about the key investment themes in the world. Some likely come so they can say they were at whatever party they attend on Saturday night. But most come to be active participants and careful listeners.

I think another reason people come has to do with the way that I organize the discussion. When I introduce a subject, I state my opinion on that subject and try to state it in the most extreme way. I try not to say anything I don't personally believe, but I try to say what I believe in a way that will provoke reactions and comments. If you listen to my introduction to each subject, you cannot help but think, "How does Byron's view differ from mine?" If I'm successful, I express it in a way different from what most people think, provoking commentary.

I've found this technique useful in other meetings. I go to many investment committee meetings where people like to talk about a subject but do not like to come to conclusions. The way to reach conclusions is to state an issue in an extreme fashion and have people react to that, and usually a conclusion will emerge from that discussion. I think that constructing a meeting with an adversarial tone can be quite useful. "Adversarial" does not need to mean "antagonistic," but directly confronting opposing views is often quite productive.

I also have a phrase that I abhor, which is when someone says, "Let me be the devil's advocate." I try to shut that person up. The devil has enough supporters; he doesn't need any outside advocates. Playing the devil's advocate typically involves unnecessary contrarianism—an argument for the sake of arguing. Good conversation requires people to express their personal opinions, hopefully backed up by facts, in good faith with one another. Or as Mike Bloomberg has put it, "In God we trust; everybody else bring data."

THE IMPORTANCE OF KEY CONNECTIONS

As a portfolio manager at Weiss, Peck & Greer, I learned firsthand the pivotal role that key connections play in shaping a successful career. At the time, Donaldson, Lufkin & Jenrette was a top institutional brokerage firm, and one of their key marketers, Charles Ellis, was instrumental in bringing together leading chief investment officers annually at the Southampton Princess Hotel in Bermuda. These gatherings were not just meetings; they were breeding grounds for lifelong friendships and career-defining opportunities.

Each year, about twenty leading portfolio managers were invited, including Julian Robertson and George Soros, to name a few. Over casual discussions that spanned from Wednesday to Sunday, we exchanged insights and challenges, fostering a community of mutual support. These connections proved invaluable. For instance, when negotiating a deal years later, I reminisced about these Bermuda meetings with a new colleague, Barton, who had joined the Lyford Cay Club in the Bahamas. Inspired, we replicated these influential gatherings in the Bahamas starting in 1985, inviting peers and their families to join. This tradition not only strengthened existing relationships but also sparked new ones. For example, I became a mentor to Ian McKinnon, who successfully managed the Ziff family's investments for years.

Networking at such events goes beyond mere acquaintance. It's about creating a web of influential individuals who can propel each other's careers forward. George Soros, with whom I developed a significant relationship over the years, often hosted gatherings at his home each summer, inviting prominent figures. These informal settings allowed us to interact with and learn from luminaries in various fields. In 1995, leveraging my connection with Soros, I facilitated his participation in a unique fireside chat at the Council on Foreign Relations. This event eschewed formal speeches in favor of a more engaging dialogue.

These experiences highlight the profound impact of nurturing relationships within your professional circle. As I benefited from these interactions—culminating in collaborative projects, like the book *Soros on Soros*, and personal gains, such as my first convertible car—so too can you. Critical strategies include engaging deeply with your peers, seeking out and creating platforms for dialogue, and fostering an environment of mutual support. They are not just for career advancement but are also for enriching your professional journey. Whether it is a formal conference or an informal dinner, every interaction is an opportunity to expand your network and, by extension, your influence and capabilities.

PRACTICAL ADVICE FOR BUILDING YOUR NETWORK

Building your network isn't always easy. It's hard to accomplish a great deal at a cocktail party. You have short interactions with many people, and it's hard to get into a detailed discussion on any particular issue. But even deepening casual friendships has its usefulness.

A dinner party with a dozen people or fewer, where you can discuss topics at great length, is most useful for getting to know someone. I don't like attending a dinner where you only interact with the person sitting next to you. I want to have a "one-table" conversation, where everyone can talk about the issues confronting each person in greater depth. If you have a group around a dinner table, they may come up with thoughtful insights that hadn't occurred to you. I attended such a party lately, and we had meaningful conversations about COVID-19, Ukraine, the economy, the dysfunction of Congress, prospects for the next midterm and presidential elections, and others.

We didn't discuss where people would spend their winters or one another's latest golf scores. And for that reason, that's the kind of party I find most enjoyable and most useful. So there are uncountable benefits of networking. But in keeping with the theme of this book, it's necessary to acknowledge that there are risks to doing this too. Every relationship—whether platonic, romantic, or professional—entails taking on some level of personal risk.

When you let someone into your life and really let them know you, you also open yourself up to the possibility of getting burned. Before you even get to that point, there is also a risk associated with putting yourself out there in the first place. Whenever you reach out to someone in an attempt to expand your circle of friends or professional acquaintances, you expose yourself to the chance of being ignored, strung along, or rejected outright. None of these are enjoyable experiences.

There's also a risk to your reputation when you put yourself out there. Perhaps you attend or host a dinner party and commit a faux pas that impacts people's impression of you. If you are conversing with someone, you could offend or insult them, perhaps accidentally and completely unknown to you, but it would hurt your reputation with that person anyway. Let's also not gloss over the fact that some people are less comfortable in social interactions, people for whom casual or serious conversation does not come easily and who get anxious around people they are not well acquainted with. For that person, there is a risk to one's sense of well-being.

When building your network and becoming integrated into various social groups, you will often be introduced through someone already a member of these circles. Another meaningful way you can do this is by reaching out to people yourself. For example, when you read about someone or go to a lecture and hear someone speak, don't be afraid to call them directly if you think they might be a person you want to include in your circle. I've done this with many people, and it's how I built my relationships with people like Bill Ackman, John Paulson, and others.

Don't be afraid to make the cold call.

Contact somebody and say, "I would like to get to know you better and exchange ideas with you." Then invite them out to lunch. I've had very few turndowns while doing this. It's worth noting that you may need to achieve personal prominence before you can connect with people this way. The person you contact might not take your call if he doesn't recognize your name. I probably couldn't have done this until I was well known at Morgan Stanley and relatively advanced in my career. Even so, it is advantageous to you, personally and professionally, to constantly think about whom you might want to connect with and be bold in trying to make it happen.

With young people tending to be more risk averse than previous generations, this topic is more important today than ever. Millennials are less likely than prior generations to be involved in political and religious institutions, be physically intimate, or get married.[2] No doubt, the rise and prevalence of social media plays a significant role

---

2   "Millennials in Adulthood: Detached from Institutions, Networked with Friends," Pew Research Center, March 7, 2014, https://www.pewresearch.org/social-trends/2014/03/07/millennials-in-adulthood/.

in this, as people are increasingly interacting with each other from behind their screens—sometimes anonymously, sometimes not. How much easier it is to chat with someone online, where you can disconnect at the first sense of discomfort or potential danger, than to excuse yourself to leave a dinner conversation turned sour.

Despite the personal risks associated with attempting to expand and nurture one's circle of acquaintances and friends, it is one of the most critical things one must do in life. The benefits are countless, as more than a fifty-five-year track record of networking demonstrates. Consider my ninetieth birthday party, which one of my dearest and longest friends, Rick Reiss, threw for me in February 2023. I have been friends with some people in attendance for nearly sixty years. Just think of that: six decades of knowing someone. That's two-thirds of my life, and the multiplicative effect can be astounding. There were around twenty people in attendance at that particular intimate dinner party, and let's assume, conservatively, that I had known the people in that room for an average of twenty-five years. That's five hundred years of cumulative friendship and love in a single room. What a reward for a lifetime of nurturing one's network.

So what is some practical advice for nurturing one's network? I've amassed some useful tips and tricks over the years. They do not completely mitigate the risks that I've discussed above. Still, they can help you navigate this sometimes difficult process, setting you up for success in achieving the broadest and deepest network that you can manage.

Practical Tips

Another one of my Life's Lessons is that when meeting someone new, one should try to find out what formative experience occurred in their lives before they were seventeen. For example, the loss of my parents when I was young was a formative experience in my life.

Most of my memories of my father were during the times of his life when he was not in good health. Finally, his health declined to a point of no return. During the last week of my father's life, when I was nine years old, he was in the Michael Reese Hospital in Chicago. My mother, who knew he was dying, wanted to spend the week with him. As I was only nine, I was too young to be left alone, and I stayed with a friend, Cuck Cole, overnight in the building.

Each morning, I would go back to our family's apartment to get a change of clothes and leave my laundry. My mother was never there because she was at the hospital with my father. But on a Thursday, I opened the front door, and my mother was there, and I knew that my father had died. As soon as I saw her, I asked, "Is Daddy dead?" And she said, "Yes." So I turned to Chuck and said, "I guess I won't be going to school today."

My mother took ill around 1945. I recall that on the night my mother passed away, I was already asleep. My mother was in an oxygen tent, and in the middle of the night, I heard some commotion, but I didn't know what it was all about. Then I heard the nurse saying, "I can't tell you," meaning she couldn't officially say that my mother had died. When I woke up the next morning, I got the bad news.

From the time I was fifteen, I was on my own and had to make all my decisions. My older brother got involved occasionally, but really, every decision about the direction of my life had to be made by me. Part of why I have such a strong memory from this time is because every decision was vivid in my mind. I had only one clear goal: to survive the difficulties I was facing.

Once my mother took sick, my maiden aunt Rose came and lived with us to help with me and my older brother and to be the caregiver for my mother. Occasionally, Aunt Rose would get invited to dinner parties, but since we couldn't afford babysitters, she would bring me along. Having eaten before, I would do my homework in another room during the dinner party. But I was always curious, and when there was an opportunity, I would try to listen to the conversation that was going on with the adults.

At one party, at the home of a man named Joe Frank, I remember him saying, "Too bad about that kid. No mother, no father, no money. No opportunity in the world. I wonder what's going to become of that kid." The implication was that whatever happened, it wouldn't be good. I remember thinking, "I'm going to prove Joe Frank wrong." And to some extent, I have.

Throughout my life, I have had many people suggest that my background as an orphan motivated me and was a reason for my success. I have a different perspective. Being orphaned made me prone to avoiding excessive risks. It's probably why I never became an entrepreneur or had any job where I worked on my own. Perhaps I would have gone further in life had I not experienced this adversity as a young man. We cannot know the counterfactual. However, knowing this information about my background can give great insight into my personality, life choices, and risk tolerance. I think that lesson is broadly applicable.

For other people, their "formative experiences" are less dramatic than mine. The seminal experience could take a variety of shapes and forms, whether it was having an influential mentor or an experience playing on a high school or college sports team. It could be flunking a course, getting expelled from school, or not getting into school in the first place. Ask people what their experience growing up was like. My human resources department is always a little uneasy when I give this advice, but I will keep giving it anyway. You will really get an insight into someone's risk tolerance by learning about incidents that happened to them in their formative years.

TREAT OTHERS AS FRIENDS FROM THE START

This brings me to another one of my Life's Lessons: When you meet someone new, treat that person as a friend. Assume he or she is a winner and will become a positive force in your life. Most people wait for others to prove their value. Give them the benefit of the doubt from the start. Occasionally, you will be disappointed, but your network will broaden rapidly if you follow this path.

Most people are suspicious of new encounters. It is so easy to put your trust in somebody and have them disappoint you, but I think you should take that risk. Most people you meet in business will be good people, not people who want to trick you. If you meet a schemer, there are characteristics that are generally revealed early in the encounter that will make you suspicious.

For the first forty years of my life, I waited for somebody to prove they could be trusted before I gave them my full confidence. I am now more likely to trust them right at the beginning and take the potential consequences, assuming they will be responsible people who treat me fairly. I think that's worked out well. I've been burned a few times, sometimes seriously, but my circle of friends and acquaintances expanded enormously once I began to trust people from my first encounter with them.

Being cynical about issues is a good idea;
being cynical about people is not.

People can tell whether you are treating them as an acquaintance or a friend.

Another life lesson of mine is that when someone extends kindness to you, write them a handwritten note, not an email. Handwritten notes make an impact and are not quickly forgotten. I'm a real believer in handwritten notes. I send many emails, but there's nothing like the impact of a handwritten note for someone who has done a special favor for you. So I use physical notes extensively.

Along with this, I've tried to become a more secure person. As one of my Life Lessons says, younger people are naturally insecure and tend to overplay their accomplishments. Most people don't become comfortable with who they are until they're in their forties. By that time, they can underplay their achievements and become nicer, more likable people. So try to get to that point as soon as you can.

When I was younger, I tried to talk a lot about myself and convince people how terrific I was. I'm different now because I've managed to perform well enough that my accomplishments can hopefully speak for themselves. It should be your goal to reach a place where you don't need to toot your own horn, and your work will influence people in your orbit to recognize you and speak favorably of you to others.

THE MOST IMPORTANT NETWORK: MY WIFE AND FAMILY

During my teenage years, I was adjusting to my new reality as someone who was largely on my own in the world and responsible for my fate. One thing that stands out about this time is that I was everybody's "extra ticket"—whenever someone had another ticket for a baseball game or a Chicago Bears football game. While I appreciated that, it seemed like I was always a part of someone else's family, and I felt bad about not having a family of my own.

While my parents were both alive, we did some things together, but because my father was ill for much of my childhood, we didn't have a normal family life. After my father died, my mother tried to provide activities for us, but both my brother and I sought family support outside the home.

So I learned much about the importance of families from those who welcomed me into their lives when I was younger. I had multiple girlfriends as a young man, and they often included me in their family activities. I yearned for that and felt it was important and missing in my life. That was one side. The other side was that it made me apprehensive about families. While I enjoy having children around me, I think my own experience as an orphan is a significant reason why I never had children of my own. The fact that I was without parents concerned me about becoming one myself. I didn't want to take the chance that I would die early and leave my children without one or both of their parents. That's what I thought, and it was not a happy circumstance.

Despite never having children, I am blessed with a remarkable extended family, particularly my wife and life partner, Anita. I met her when I was a portfolio manager at Brokaw, where she was also working. Though it had been years since we worked together, I had always remembered her as an attractive, intelligent lady. Anita was born in New York but spent her formative years in Germany. Her parents, Hermann and Hilda Volz, emigrated from Germany in 1928, settling in New York. Hermann joined a bank that later merged with Chase Bank. Several years after the end of World War II, he was transferred to Germany to reopen Chase's branches. The bank had received a concession to provide banking services to American military forces based there, an assignment that developed into an extended stay. So from when she was eight years old until she was seventeen, Anita lived in Frankfurt.

Anita went to Smith and received her MBA from New York University, taking classes at night. After she graduated from college, she worked for three years in Paris. Having lived in Germany and France, she is fluent in German and French, making her a tremendous travel companion for our Europe trips, and we have had countless delightful trips to Paris together. She has had a distinguished professional career at the G7 Group, now known as Observatory Group. She partnered with Jane Hartley, who later became US ambassador to both France and the UK, and the firm provides consulting services on economic and political issues to financial institutions.

In Anita, I found a real partner in every sense of the word. We have a rich intellectual life together, but we have had a lot of fun, whether traveling or attending events. We discuss important ideas related to investment and politics, and while we have a lot of differences of opinions—especially on political issues, where she tends to be more progressive than I am—these have also provided us with lots of good conversation and the sharpening of each other's ideas. I have relied on Anita throughout the years, and she has greatly helped me in my career. There isn't an essay I write that I don't ask her to review with her keen eye. She has also kept me from doing some foolish things, and she has encouraged me to take risks in my career.

Anita has also been instrumental in some of my biggest life decisions. For example, I didn't own any real estate until I was fifty-nine. One day, Anita presented me with a piece of paper divided into two columns. In the first column were items including the cost of buying an apartment, refurbishing and furnishing it, and the total. In the other column was the cost of a divorce. She said, "Here, you went to Harvard Business School. Which column looks better to you?" We began to look for apartments.

We finally settled on a unit on Park Avenue, about two blocks from our rent-stabilized, two-bedroom, one-bathroom apartment on the third floor of a walk-up building. I bid three-quarters of the asking price, but the real estate agent said the seller found that unacceptable and that if I truly wanted the apartment, I would have to bid the full asking price, which I did. Happily, for me and my marriage, we got the apartment.

All the good things that have happened in my life since I was in my forties are because of Anita. Not only do we have a lot of interests in common, but we also tend to react to people similarly. Most of our friends are our friends in common. She is often close to the female counterpart, and I'm close to the male. We like to do the same things. We enjoy travel, the theater, concerts, and sports. She is a very good tennis player and even won the club championship in the early 1980s. She still looks incredible, even though she's in her eighties, and she's the envy of many women in the Hamptons, and for good reason. I'm sure plenty of people wonder what she sees in me, but I plan to keep them wondering.

I am also very close to my nephews, both my brother's son, Mike Wien, and his two boys, Jason and Andrew. They have substituted for children and grandchildren for me. (I find it worth mentioning that I have never changed a diaper, and I don't particularly regret that.)

CHAPTER 4

THERE'S A PERFECT JOB FOR EVERYONE

There is a perfect job out there for everyone. Most people never find it. Keep looking. The goal of life is to be a happy person, and the right job is essential to that.

During my undergraduate studies, I majored in chemistry and physics. I wanted to keep the option open to go to medical school. But in my senior year, I spent a few days at the law school and proceeded to fall asleep in class (not a good sign). At medical school, I decided I didn't really want to deal with patients one-on-one. But the business school intrigued me. So I decided to apply to Harvard Business School (HBS).

Students at Harvard live in residential houses, and I was friendly with the tutor of Dunster House, Stan Miles. In my senior year, I was convinced that, despite my good grades and my assumed board scores, because I was young, didn't have business or army experience, and was applying directly from college, HBS would turn me down.

One day in the spring of 1954, I walked over to the admissions office of HBS across the Charles and asked to see the dean of admissions, explaining that I was an applicant for the class of 1956. The secretary asked me to wait a moment. She came back and said that the dean could not see me but that someone in the admissions office would give me an interview. After I waited some more, someone from the admissions department invited me into his office. He interviewed me, and I explained that I had been working since high school, so I was ready for business school right out of college. The admissions officer explained that they like admitting people with more experience, but he would record my interest.

After my meeting, I went back to the Dunster House dining room and happened to sit with the senior tutor, Stan Miles. He asked me what I had done that day, and I explained that I was concerned that I wouldn't get into the business school and had gone to plead my case.

Miles responded, "You know, Byron, during your undergraduate years, you've done many dumb things, but this might be the dumbest. You were a clear candidate to be accepted. But by doing something so immature as to go over there and plead your case, you probably jeopardized your chances. We will see how it turns out, but if you had asked me, I would have advised you not to do that." Thankfully, Miles was wrong. I was accepted to HBS, and I enrolled the following fall of 1954.

THE RISK PAYS OFF

I probably did not know how big a risk I was taking when I strode into the admissions office that day, but taking that initiative may have been just what put me over the top. My first thirty years had been about survival, adjusting to my new reality as a person responsible for my fate at a young age, and ultimately, finding my way in the world. I made great strides toward this latter goal during my college and graduate school years. They allowed me to travel, make important relationships that would benefit me both personally and professionally, and learn a lot about my talents and interests.

I was no longer the young orphan who was navigating the dangers and hardships that were thrust upon me. I was now a double graduate of Harvard, with immense opportunity and, more importantly, the desire to make something of myself. Some amount of it may have been to prove the naysayers wrong. But as I've mentioned, I don't attribute my success primarily to my status as an orphan. I have always been ambitious and hardworking, and I viewed not having parents as a significant setback in achieving that success. But I refused to use this as an excuse.

My next thirty years can be described as my journey of navigating various jobs and industries in search of something that would make me happy and by which I could achieve the financial independence I had always sought. In doing so, I could create the home and community I so desperately missed as the "extra ticket" in everyone else's family. If my first three decades were about treading water to keep myself from drowning, the next three decades were about learning to swim so I could move forward in life.

I was a B-player overall who sought to become an A-player at something. I hadn't quite discovered what it was yet, but I knew I had the diligence to find it, the dedication to excel at it, and the creativity to set myself apart. In the process, I have forged the family I so deeply desired all my life and formed incredible relationships along the way. I also have some interesting stories about the life and times of over a half century of working on Wall Street.

But as you will see, this was a challenging journey. The road was winding, and the path was never linear. There were many detours and road bumps before reaching the destination. And even once I got there, I realized that the destination was less of a finish line and more of a stop on a longer journey. So if you are interested in how someone at a crossroads can find their niche, read on.

EXPERIMENTING WITH CAREER PATHS

When I left business school, I was interested in advertising because I thought I could write and be in business simultaneously. By then, I knew I wouldn't be a writer for a living, but I enjoyed it as an element of my job. The prime job in 1956 was Foote, Cone & Belding, the ad agency that had won the Edsel new car account at Ford. Everyone in marketing at HBS wanted that job, and the competition was fierce.

There was a series of interviews in Boston and Chicago (where the company was based, unlike most other big agencies headquartered in New York). I competed for the job and was one of two selected people. So in June 1956, I went to work for Foote, Cone & Belding. It turned out to be a work culture that could have suited me better. The people were somewhat superficial, and it was a hard place to get ahead. When something good happened, eight people took credit for it, but when something bad happened, junior people took the blame.

I did not stay long at Foote, Cone & Belding because, in February 1957, I was drafted into the army. When I graduated from business school, I was offered a commission as a second lieutenant in the Quartermaster Corps. Still, I turned it down because it would require serving for three years, which was longer than I wanted to commit to. Upon being drafted, I was sent to Fort Leonard Wood for basic training. It was the worst place I had ever been in the United

States. They must have had a lever there where the temperature went from twenty degrees in April to ninety degrees, seemingly overnight. It was muddy and dirty, and the barracks were heated with coal. The coal dust filled the air nonstop. When cadets were allowed to leave the base and go to the movies, everyone in the theater could be heard coughing continuously. It was a terrible experience, but after basic training, we were assigned to a permanent location for the next twenty-one months.

My permanent assignment was to the Quartermaster Research and Engineering Command in Natick, Massachusetts, about twenty miles outside of Boston. Natick was primarily a civilian research facility, and I was assigned there because my military and occupational specialty rating classification was "scientific and professional." I was sent to this facility to work in the laboratory and work on parachute quality. As part of this assignment, I spent a month in Fort Lee, Virginia, testing parachutes.

I spent most of my time in the laboratory room, which we called the "OK Corral." It turned out that somebody who had some money and was an investor worked at the research facility. He and I spent much of our free time talking about investments, which is where my interest in investment management was kindled. We subscribed to *Value Line* and other financial publications. His name was Hyman Shrager, and I consider him one of my greatest mentors.

Despite the living conditions, I enjoyed my army experience. It was an eight-hour-a-day, five-day-a-week job. I played tennis and learned how to ski when I wasn't working. I often told my army buddies that it would be the best two years of my life. I don't think it was that, but it was certainly a good time. I was in the army with enough money, my room and board paid for, and $85 to spend on what I wanted (younger readers will have to take my word for it that this was actually a generous sum in those days), and I really enjoyed the experience.

I got out of the army in February 1959. Fred Leiner, my first-year roommate in business school, had been working for the Armour Research Foundation, the management consulting division of the Illinois Institute of Technology. They did primarily management consulting in scientific areas, and my undergraduate experience in chemistry and physics and my business school experience made me an ideal candidate. Employees there were paid university salaries, and I started there at $7,500 a year, which is about what I would have been making at Foote Cone if I had gone back after the army. I thought management consulting might be a better fit for me.

Armour Research got interesting assignments, one of which was the industrial revitalization of the state of Maine, which at that time had been primarily in the textile and shoe manufacturing businesses. Companies in those industries were either moving south or abroad, so the state of Maine hired the consultancy to help them with a rein-dustrialization plan, and I was assigned to that project. I traveled all throughout Maine, visiting companies and working on that project.

Armour Research also got a project from the Rockefellers Brothers Fund to work on the industrial development of Nigeria. In 1960, Nigeria became an independent country (it had been a British pro-tectorate), and they were trying to think of ways to take advantage of their natural resources to create more jobs for the forty million people who lived there then. At the time, it was the most populous country between Egypt and South Africa. The leadership of that project was in the hands of Armour Research, and the people on the project were going to partner with the Electric Storage Battery (Exide) company. The town of Abeokuta in eastern Nigeria had lead deposits, and they wanted to develop their storage battery capability so they could manufacture storage batteries for all of Africa and avoid the heavy shipping costs from Europe.

None of the senior people at Armour wanted to go to Nigeria for this project, so I volunteered, even though I had only been there a year. Faced with the choice of sending my novice self or turning down the project, they chose to send me. Three weeks before I left for this trip, I had married my first wife, Lois Rosenthal, a woman I had met while I was at business school and living in Chicago. We got married in August 1960, and I flew out to Africa a month later, in September 1960. The country was set to become independent in November later that year.

While traveling to Nigeria, I flew from New York to London on my first jet airplane. From there, I took a prop plane to Tripoli, Libya, and then continued to Lagos. I traveled all over Nigeria and developed an interest in African art that still stays with me. I visited every region, experiencing many small towns and villages. It was a terrific experience. I was there for about a month, and when my project was complete, I left for my honeymoon in Portugal. We connected in Lisbon and spent several weeks in the country before returning to Chicago. I stayed at Armour Research for two years.

MY ENTRÉE INTO FINANCE

After HBS, I contacted people from my graduating class to see if any of them might know of a job for me, and that was how I ended up at Brokaw, Schaenen and Clancy. Bill Brokaw remembered me from HBS and offered me a job as a security analyst, thus beginning my introduction to the investment business in 1965.

Bill Brokaw was an enormously talented investor. He was intuitive rather than analytical, but he had an exceptional way of picking stocks. He was also a manic-depressive, and he could be violent at times. During the period I was there, from 1965 through 1974, his psychological problems became serious, and eventually, he left the firm. In 1973, the market was difficult. A bear market was going on because of the recession that occurred in 1973 and 1974, and the Employee Retirement Income Security Act of 1974 was passed.

We didn't have the critical mass to compete for institutional business, so we felt we had to merge with another firm. Nelson Schaenen had gone to Cornell and was friendly with a fellow Cornell alum, Stephen Weiss, of Weiss, Peck & Greer. They decided their two firms should merge and worked out a deal to do so. Weiss would move into our offices at 30 Wall Street, and several of us would be partners, including Schaenen and Clancy. But at the last minute, Clancy decided he didn't want to go to a firm where his name wouldn't be on the door, and he resigned. So Schaenen and I went to work at Weiss, Peck & Greer as partners.

During my years as a security analyst at Brokaw, Schaenen and Clancy, I analyzed the operations of dozens of companies. Two cases from the 1970s were notable. Bausch & Lomb had developed a soft contact lens, representing a real breakthrough. Our firm had created a large position in the stock, and Dick Clancy and I made frequent trips to Rochester, New York, to speak with executives there. We sensed a less optimistic mood on our final trip, although we were given no specific negative information to support it. As a result, we began to sell the stock. The Securities and Exchange Commission took the position that the sale was made based on inside information. We eventually settled the case without admitting to or denying guilt in an administrative action. Ten years later, when I was at Morgan Stanley, the firm moved to vacate that action and was successful in doing so.

The other encounter with the SEC involved another Rochester-area company, Stirling Homex. This company was brought to our attention by Ken Langone, who was with R.W. Pressprich and later became one of the founders of Home Depot. We became friendly with Ken through our involvement in Electronic Data Systems, Ross Perot's company. Pressprich had taken Electronic Data Systems public at one hundred times earnings, and the Stirling brothers wanted to do the same.

The company was a manufacturer of modular housing units, and we took a prominent position in the stock. Demand for the product was strong, but deliveries were slow. At one point in October, the chief financial officer assured us that delivery modular units being stored at the company would be shipped to customers who had committed to buy them by year-end. Shortly after the beginning of the year, Dick Clancy and I flew to Rochester and chartered a small single-propeller plane to fly over Stirling's Avon, New York, storage lot to count the modular units.

Heavy snow had fallen overnight, accentuating the lines that separated the modular units from one another in the lot. The plane made seven passes over the lot, and we determined that virtually all the units had yet to be delivered, as promised. We liquidated our position, and the company went bankrupt several months after receiving a loan from Merrill Lynch. The SEC inquired of us, thinking this might be another case of so-called insider information.

We explained that the sale decision was made based on the surveillance flight and was, quite literally, "outside information." The SEC accepted that.

Earlier in my career, we had a standard procedure when I was covering industries and specific companies. We would identify a company that looked interesting for investment and collect the research reports from the various brokerage firms that covered that company. If it looked like an attractive investment, we planned an on-site visit to the company. We spent a lot of time on such field trips. As I reflect on it, I don't know how much value we consistently derived from these experiences. While we prepared our questions carefully, the company was often quite adept at deflecting the penetrating questions. They were more proficient at it than we were in recognizing that that's what they were doing. So the field trips were of questionable utility much of the time.

I know a lot of money managers who never visit companies and do very well. I also know a lot of quality money managers who know the symbol of a company but don't know the name of a company or what it does, and they do very well too. So before you buy a plane ticket and get a hotel for the trip, make sure you know what you will get out of it because it may be more trouble than it's worth.

I was a portfolio manager when I joined Weiss, Peck & Greer and was doing well for my accounts. My compensation was increasing; by 1982, I was playing a strategy role for the firm. We were going through a bear market, and I helped the firm position itself defensively. More importantly, in 1982, near the bottom of the market decline, I became aggressively positive, and we took advantage of it. At the end of 1982, I didn't think I was rewarded adequately for my role in developing the firm's strategy and our success.

At that time, I had a good friend who had formed a small money management firm, Century Capital. Jim Harpel had gone to Harvard, as I had, but he didn't finish. He was so smart that he got into HBS without graduating from college. While in business school, he was recruited to be the chief financial officer of a company in the coin-operated amusement business. His business and my business were similar. We had met at an HBS gathering and had become friends.

When I moved to New York, he moved too. He went to work for Wertheim and was a successful money manager there. He teamed up with another wealthy Chicagoan, Richard Hokin, and formed Century Capital, which was correct in predicting the downturn of 1973–74 and got a lot of business from institutions as a result. By that time, Jim and I had become very friendly. He married Diana Kann, the daughter of a wealthy retailer in Baltimore. It was a very extravagant wedding on a weekend in late November, and I was an usher.

Jim had invited me to join his firm almost continuously from 1981 to 1982. Since I was disappointed with my compensation at Weiss, Peck, I agreed at the beginning of 1983 to join Century Capital. One of its advantages was that it was located on Third Avenue and Forty-Eighth Street, and I wouldn't have to take the subway downtown for my commute. At the end of the first year that I was at the firm, Jim and his partner, Richard Hokin, sold almost half of the firm's total interest to the Belzberg family of Canada, making them a minority general partner. The idea was that we would help them manage their family money and hopefully grow the business on our own.

In the recovery afterward, Jim lost interest in money management and decided to leave the firm in 1984 to sell his remaining interest. Richard went along with the sale. They negotiated the transaction without telling any of the other partners, which they could do because together they had a majority interest. Jim knew if he had told me, I would have been against the deal because I had joined Century to help build it out and hopefully make my life fortune. He sold his interest and converted the Belzbergs from a minority junior partner to a majority general partner.

Eventually, the Belzbergs amassed 76 percent interest in the firm and were able to push out the remaining partners, which they did. I had a 10 percent stake in the firm, for which I received about $1 million. Under the original 1983 deal with the Belzbergs, I had to sign an employment contract that lasted three years and was precluded from working for another firm. When they bought a controlling interest, I was released from the contract with the help of my lawyer's intervention.

TRANSITION TO STRATEGY

By then, Morgan Stanley had approached me to become the strategist for the United States, and I had already been considering that job. During my time at Brokaw, Schaenen and Clancy, and particularly at Weiss, Peck, I changed my role from security analyst to portfolio manager. I was successful in the latter, having started to build a reputation for myself doing investment strategy. I began to establish a friendship with Barton Biggs, a strategist at Morgan Stanley, and I would have periodic lunches with him.

At one of the lunches, we discussed investment opportunities— which stocks were working and why. Then Barton said he wanted to change the subject. He was becoming the head of Morgan Stanley Investment Management; he was going to be the global strategist, and he needed someone to be the US strategist. Barton assured me that the research department, management committee, and sales department had met and decided I would be perfect for the job. (I later learned I was the seventh person they had approached with that line.)

All my life as a portfolio manager, I had thought there must be something better than this. I realized that managing money was a short-term goal for me. It was easy to burn out doing it, but something even more critical didn't sit well with me. I recall that at one Christmas party, someone asked me, "How are you doing?" and I said, "I'm doing well." They replied, "That's not what I meant; how much are you up for the year?" I told them, "21 percent," and I realized when I got home that night that I wasn't a person but a number.

I didn't want to be a number anymore.

Being a portfolio manager requires you to be focused on your portfolio twenty-four hours a day, seven days a week, and I couldn't do that much longer. Morgan Stanley came to me with the opportunity to be a strategist, and there were elements of that job that I had always wanted. The first was that I would be able to write every week, and I could count on being published. When I was in college, everyone told me I was a good writer, but I didn't see myself spending my career that way. I was fortunate that John Updike was a classmate, and I would read his work in the *Lampoon* and realize that he was a writer—I was a hack.

But I wanted to write, which was part of why I went to work for an ad agency right out of business school. I didn't like that, which is one reason why I went to work for a management consulting firm. I could write reports there, but I would not be a "writer." Suddenly, Morgan Stanley offered me a job where I could write and be in business, and that had always been my objective.

I went to Lee Cooperman, who was the Goldman Sachs strategist at the time, and told him that I thought I would be offered this job at Morgan Stanley. I asked him what he thought about it. He said I would be crazy to take it and told me, "Being a strategist is a terrible job. You have to write all the time, travel all over the country to see clients, and you're on the sales side. You're a successful portfolio manager; why would you want to change?"

I remember going home and thinking about it and realizing if I became a strategist, it would enable me to do the things I had wanted to do all my life. I could write every week, get published, and travel to places I had never been, like Japan and China. I could meet with portfolio managers in Europe, where I had primarily been as a tourist. I discussed it with another classmate of mine from HBS. He said, "You'll be thinking about it, and there will be a birdie on your shoulder telling you whether you should take the job or not."

The birdie told me to take the job. One of the things Cooperman said was, "You don't know whether you'll be successful or not. What if you fail at it? How will you get back into money management?" But I decided it was worth the risk, and I went to work at Morgan Stanley in January 1985. It led to a whole new career that has been enormously fulfilling and satisfying to me.

During the negotiation with Morgan Stanley, there was a bait-and-switch circumstance. All the time I was talking with Barton about joining the firm as a US strategist, the understanding was that I would join as a managing director, which meant I would be a partner at Morgan Stanley, which, back in 1984, was still a private partnership. The job offer came in December, and at that time, Morgan Stanley was considering promoting principals to manager directors. They were going to make me a managing director, someone from outside the firm who had never proven his ability within the firm. One committee member pointed out that while I was a successful portfolio manager, I had never been a strategist. They didn't know whether I had the right skills, such as writing, or whether I would be accepted thoroughly by the clients or any other important constituents of a US strategist.

How could they promote this unproven quantity and deprive those who had done well in investment banking of a promotion?

Barton was obliged to inform me that the firm was still offering me the job but not the partnership. I told him immediately that I wasn't interested in the deal unless I could become a partner, and he said he understood but encouraged me to think it over. I realized that the job, if I succeeded, would be more satisfying than anything I had ever done.

So I went to Barton and told him I understood the firm's position and would join the firm with no title other than "Byron Wien, US strategist." I thought that at the end of the year, I would have done well or failed at the job; in this case, I would leave and collect my salary and any bonus the firm chose to give me. But if I succeeded, I would like to be made whole. In other words, I would like to have the number of partnership points (equity ownership) I would have had if I had joined as a partner in 1985. Barton returned and talked with the Management Committee, and they agreed to that deal. It ended up being worth millions of dollars because I had jumped ahead of my class regarding equity ownership. That was particularly important in 1986, when the firm went public.

Morgan Stanley wanted to go public because it was becoming a global firm, and it took more work to replenish the capital of the retiring partners and have enough capital to expand its global operations. There were many controversies when Wall Street firms began to go public, which started in 1970 when Donaldson, Lufkin & Jenrette went public but really intensified in the 1980s when Morgan Stanley went public and Goldman Sachs followed.

In my judgment, the major investment banking firms didn't have sufficient capital from the working partners to sustain a global business, so they had to raise outside capital. Remaining private was a conceit. A small firm could be profitable but would never have the capital resources to expand the business in a significant way internationally. The fact that most of these firms are public now, I think, has probably improved the sustainability of the investment banking business and the quality of the output. However, the willingness to take on risk has certainly increased because bad decisions mean that partners are losing other people's money, not their own.

Morgan Stanley was considered one of the preeminent investment banking firms at the time, along with Kuhn, Loeb & Co.; Dillon, Read & Company; and White, Weld & Co. Goldman Sachs was not yet considered to be in the top tier. It turned out to be a significant step for me and changed my life.

Barton took a big chance on me; it must have been intuitive. He hired me as a strategist even though he had never seen anything I had written, and he trusted my investment judgment without much evidence. He was an excellent writer and thinker, and I learned much from him. We socialized and played tennis together but never really became very close. Once, I told him that I wanted to talk to him about "our relationship." Barton, being the tough ex-Marine that he was, didn't think that men had relationships with each other. He said, "I never want you to say that to me again." And I never did.

I began writing a weekly essay about the market, even as Barton did the same. He wrote more on international issues, and I focused on domestic ones, given my role as a US strategist. Very often, Barton's content would creep into my territory. I didn't mind it, though, because he had good insights, and there was always more than enough for the both of us to analyze in any given week.

I started traveling to visit accounts almost from the first day I was on the job. I wasn't known outside New York's aggressive money management circles. I had participated in many stock market discussion groups and was well known in that community, but I wasn't known particularly outside the city.

From 1985 until after 2000, my work at Morgan Stanley was grueling, but I loved it. I wrote an eleven-hundred-word essay every week, even when I went on vacation. I traveled extensively, generally about two weeks a month, visiting US, Europe, and Asia clients. I loved every minute of it, but it took all my time. I had to devote some part of every weekend to writing. We had a house in the Hamptons during that period and often returned to the city late on Sunday evening. It was not uncommon for me to finish my weekly essay after dinner and not go to bed until 2:00 a.m. Then I would have to attend the Monday morning meeting at 8:00 a.m.

My grueling schedule at Morgan Stanley paid off. As my interaction with Pat Trunzo showed, I was beginning to develop a reputation, both inside the financial world and beyond. It didn't come easy, though. I had spent my "ten thousand hours" and then some. Barton was writing every week also, and he had a much more visible profile than I did, but bit by bit, I began to develop a following. My first two "fans," as it were, were Larry Tisch of the Loews Corporation and Marvin Schwartz at Neuberger Berman. They were both widely respected in the industry and told others they should read my work. That was a big help in the beginning.

Most clients responded well to what I was doing, but one person I needed help with was the CIO at the University of Wisconsin, which was an important client. Eventually, I convinced him, too, by directly confronting him. He said he wouldn't see me, but I begged for an appointment. I went to Madison to meet him, eventually winning him over. That's an example of how persistence and direct communication with someone can win the day. When someone doesn't appreciate your work, don't be afraid to confront them directly.

As I honed my skills and developed my reputation, I transitioned from a B-player to an A-player. I had ascended to a chief strategist role at one of the preeminent investment banks, but I noticed what it took to get there. My path wasn't linear, and I tried multiple career avenues, adjusting as necessary to find my niche, where I could excel and ascend to the top of the ladder.

I liked being in business, but money management wasn't the right fit for me. I was successful as a portfolio manager, but I decided I had passions for writing and critical thinking that weren't met by those jobs. I also wasn't as happy as I could be. I learned that being defined by my numbers (and being defined as a number) was not how I wanted to live my life. Finally, I settled on being a strategist. Though the work was grueling, I was willing and able to dedicate the time I needed to establish a reputation for myself and, eventually, reach the profession's pinnacle.

There is something important to take away here for anyone who is a B-player but desires something greater. Don't be complacent, even if you have achieved some measure of success. Take responsibility for your failures, and work as hard as possible to correct them and become better at what you do. I did this when I turned things around as a portfolio manager at Brokaw, Schaenen and Clancy. If you are dissatisfied and think there's something better for you, be willing to try new things, even if it involves some measure of risk or is new to you, or you are unsure whether you will be any good at it. That's what I had to do to make the jump to become an investment strategist.

Employ your creativity on the job and develop a new idea that will set you apart, as I did when I developed (and fought for) the Ten Surprises at Morgan Stanley. Maintain your integrity and be willing to walk away if you have conviction about something. As you'll read, when I wrote a provocative piece that angered senior management, it wasn't easy for me, but it was an important milestone in my life that garnered me respect from influential people.

Finally, never stop reinventing yourself. Even though I had become an A-player as an investment strategist, I was not willing to retire or to take a step back, partially because I felt I still had value to contribute but also because once I found my niche in the world, the idea of stepping away was simply unfathomable. I found what I loved to do, and I imagine I'll let it kill me before I am willing to let it go.

Another important aspect of finding your perfect job involves an insistence on doing what's right and sticking to your guns, even when it's hard. As another of my Life's Lessons says, the hard way is always the right way. Never take shortcuts, except when driving home from the Hamptons. Shortcuts can be construed as sloppiness, a career killer.

In 2001, before the infamous Enron or MCI scandals, I began to worry about the culture of American business, whether prominent companies were taking shortcuts in their business practices or otherwise acting in unadmirable ways. I wrote an essay called "The Issue of Integrity." It essentially made the point (this was before "ESG" issues rose to prominence) that adhering to high moral principles was a responsibility of every chief executive. I felt that several business leaders weren't paying attention to the importance of that, and they had a responsibility to their customers, suppliers, employees, and investors.

Upon reviewing the piece, my editor at Morgan Stanley (who was ostensibly there to check language and spelling) thought it was too controversial. He presented it to the management of the firm, worried that they would be unsettled by my statement that there were companies in finance who were guilty of some of the same transgressions that I saw taking place in other industries. Vikram Pandit, head of equities at the time, said that the essay would be too controversial and critical of financial services firms, including Morgan Stanley, even though I did not mention our firm by name. Mayree Clark, head of research, agreed with him, and they came to me and said that they weren't going to publish the essay. I reminded them that my deal with the firm was that they had to publish everything I wrote, and they could fire me after it was published. But they would not relent.

I told them, "I'm going to quit, and as a visible person by now, I think the *New York Times* or *Wall Street Journal* will come to me and say, 'We thought you loved Morgan Stanley; why are you quitting?' And I will say I wrote an essay called—and pay close attention to the title—'The Issue of Integrity,' and Morgan Stanley refused to print it. I don't think that's going to play very well." My superiors told me I couldn't do that because they owned my writing. I said, "No, you don't; you only own it if you publish it!" They told me they would get back to me and eventually decided to publish the essay.

The piece was widely read and even more widely distributed. Right after it was published, Arthur Rock, a technology venture capitalist and an important advisor to Intel and Apple, emailed me, saying he would like to meet me. I knew he was a regular skier in Aspen, and I told him I went there often and would make arrangements to see him once when we were both out there. I went to Aspen that spring and met him for dinner, and he and his wife became excellent friends of ours, which they remain to this day. That's a good example of treating your work with integrity; you may very well find that there are people in prominent places who will respect it.

CHAPTER 5

THE INVESTOR'S COMPASS

If you want to be successful and live a long, stimulating life, keep yourself at risk intellectually all the time.

The first step in becoming an investor is finding out what excites you.

Some people enjoy gathering an incremental understanding of simple concepts. If that sounds like you, you will likely be a value investor. You may enjoy analyzing established companies with strong franchises that can grow earnings because the public or industrial enterprises widely consume their products or services. In these cases, the next quarter's earnings make a big difference in your valuation of the firm. Value companies tend to have modest margins and more predictable earnings streams but are often more vulnerable to changes in economic and business cycles.

I am excited by innovation, which typically lends itself to a growth investing mindset. That said, it can be a tougher path because innovation always happens. The trick is figuring out what is sustainable and what is not. There are rare companies like Alphabet or Meta that have products or services that have grown sustainably with generous profit margins for a long time. But nothing lasts forever. In the famous words of economist Herb Stein, "If something cannot go on forever, it will stop." I get excited by the process of finding those exceptional businesses that are exceptions to the rule.

Even if the trajectory of growth companies is less likely to be derailed by economic cycles, the market will always have its fluctuations. What do you do when you are holding a good stock through a bear market? I think you have to equip yourself to endure the bear market and watch the stock go down. If the concept or product is sound, and the bear market ends, the stock will go back up again. If the product is not sustainable or the research process is not regenerative, that idea doesn't hold. The only way to have stocks that are compound ten to one hundred times your original investment is to hold them through bear markets, as I have done.

One of my critics says I'm just lazy. But I know I'm not smart enough to sell and buy the stock back to take advantage of the downdraft and recovery. In addition, market timing can only be practiced by a few people; it's very hard to sell a stock at the top and buy it at the bottom. So if you have an outstanding stock and a lot of conviction, buying and holding is better. If it's as good as you think, and you have done your diligence, it will do well when the market recovers.

DECIDING WHAT'S IMPORTANT (FOR YOU)

When I was younger, I often attended portfolio manager meetings organized by brokerage firms or informally by investment managers. The attendees typically fell into two categories, which I'll call the top-downers and the stock pickers. I've always identified as a top-downer.

This is someone who examines the world, analyzes the factors shaping the investment landscape, and selects stocks based on a comprehensive assessment of the economy, geopolitical dynamics, and other influences.

Everything in the world matters to me as a top-downer. I'm concerned about politics, economics, environmental factors, and geopolitical issues, and I try to consider all of these and judge what the market will do. Within that overall framework, I try to decide what sectors will perform well.

But that's a broad remit, so it can be difficult to decide what is important. Certain things will always be significant, no matter what stage of the cycle one is in. It's important to know the economic outlook, for example. Another is the direction of interest rates. Those are related because the pace of economic growth generally determines interest rates. Rates, in turn, impact valuations.

The political environment is also relevant. Historically, Democratic administrations are more likely to run budget deficits, and Republican administrations are more likely to show fiscal restraint. Government spending and borrowing affect economic growth, interest rates, and, thus, the overall investment environment. These factors are all interrelated, each impacting the other.

What is going on in the world matters too. If there is strife in parts of the world like there is today in Ukraine, it impacts economies in Europe and Asia. To understand that, you should have an understanding of the important geopolitical figures in the world. For example, China's policy direction is significant, as it trends toward being the biggest economy in the world. But you need to weigh how much each factor impacts your outlook.

Until 2022, military conflicts occurred in various parts of the world, but none had a major effect on the economy. Ukraine changed that. We didn't have to worry about pandemics over the past decade, but since 2019, COVID-19 has been an important factor across the world—changing the way people behave, including their propensity to work in offices and to travel.

Although most people return to work in traditional settings, the landscape is different. You have to understand important long-term factors, including climate change. Governments will have to commit capital to protect the environment and raise money to do that, which will impact tax policy for both individuals and corporations.

Macro factors cannot be ignored. Those who say they are "bottom-up" investors claim to only examine individual companies' issues. I think these people are not seeing the whole story. Even if you are a stock picker, you must understand the background factors that will influence your portfolio. There are no top-downers who don't have certain stock-picking characteristics. After all, you can be a macro investor and confine yourself to interest rates, currencies, and similar factors related to the economy, but that's not the way to make real money. The way to do that is to pick a stock that goes up many times. And most top-downers do own individual stocks.

Similarly, if you're a stock picker, you must engage in the work to understand the environment. If you buy into something without considering the direction of the overall markets, you can incur big losses. So the relationship between top-downers and stock pickers is important, and I don't know anyone successful in either group who doesn't have substantial contacts in the other group.

I would say I'm right more than half the time with a particular investment, but not as much as three-quarters of the time. I have to be sensitive to when I'm wrong and willing to sell a stock at a loss. But if you have a lot of winners, you can always use those winners to offset capital losses.

QUALITIES OF SUCCESSFUL INVESTORS

Having identified what excites you and what matters most in your investment journey, we can now explore the commonalities among people who have excelled in this field. No two investors are alike, but successful investors share certain qualities. These traits exist in a delicate balance that may seem contradictory at first glance.

One of the most crucial tensions lies in the realm of continuous learning. Successful investors are lifelong learners, always looking for new information and insights that could impact their investments. Yet they also understand the importance of knowing when they have enough information to make a decision. This requires an ability to filter through vast amounts of data to determine what is most relevant and actionable while avoiding the trap of overanalysis, which can lead to overconfidence or missed opportunities.

Another vital balance is between enthusiasm and emotional detachment. As discussed before, finding investments that genuinely excite you can fuel thorough research and deeper understanding. However, it's equally important to maintain objectivity and not let emotions drive your investment decisions. Emotional attachment can cloud judgment and lead to irrational choices, so successful investors must cultivate the ability to stay disciplined and make decisions based on sound analysis.

In this section, we explore how these qualities—continuous learning tempered with decisive action and passionate interest balanced with disciplined detachment—interplay to create a foundation for successful investing. Investors who master these qualities can navigate the complexities of the market and are better equipped for long-term success.

KNOWING WHEN YOU HAVE "ENOUGH"

One of the criticisms of Joe Biden as president is that he always asks for more research whenever there is a meeting about an issue. That tells me he would not be a good investor. A good investor makes significant decisions with incomplete information. This is not to minimize the importance of doing good research and gathering as much good data as possible. But at some point, investors must be able to say "I have enough"—enough to commit capital to a stock or concept even though risks and uncertainty remain. It's hard to pull the trigger in those circumstances, and it takes a certain personality to do so.

Some people are more intuitive than others, and they can tell when they have enough very early in the game. Others act based on a feeling in their gut, and others are comfortable with others' recommendations. That's not enough for me. I need to understand how a company is doing, how the products might be regenerative, how the earnings will come through, and how the margins will remain secure. I must get comfortable with all these things before I'm willing to commit. But no one is right all the time.

You must do your best to keep emotions out of your investing. It is hard to do that, especially when you are losing money. This is why building a portfolio that coincides with your risk tolerance is ideal. As your net worth increases and the portfolio becomes retirement or legacy money, keeping your emotions out of it is easier. Suppose you have a portfolio that is worth ten times the amount of your annual expenses. In that case, you likely will not overreact to a 20 percent downturn in the market because the losses would not necessarily affect your lifestyle. If you have not yet reached this level of financial security, it's important to be careful when investing.

Don't invest money you can't afford to lose, and you won't take actions that you'll be sorry about later.

The heroes of the investment world are those who let winning picks run and cut their losses. If your initial premises are proven incorrect, be willing to sell, even at a loss. Waiting for the passage of time to make you even will often result in further losses. Let your winners run, and exit losing positions as soon as you realize you're wrong. You can achieve this by constantly evaluating your investment premise: Why did you buy the stock, and is that reason still valid?

Investors must avoid falling into the trap of "thesis creep," where they alter their original rationale for an investment to align with changing circumstances, often to justify not taking a loss. This behavior can lead to substantial financial setbacks. Instead, maintain discipline by regularly reviewing your investment's core premises. Ask yourself whether the company is meeting its goals and continuing to show growth potential, and whether its strategic initiatives remain on track. If the answers to these critical questions are negative, it's essential to recognize that clinging to a failing investment due to emotional attachment or sunk-cost fallacy will only exacerbate losses. Rational decision-making and adherence to your initial investment criteria are vital for long-term success.

For example, if you buy a pharmaceutical company, ensure it can regenerate its product line. A profitable product will likely be replicated by generics or competitors, so the company must have a pipeline of new products to enrich its portfolio. Perhaps you bought a company like this and were excited by its plans for product development. It will be critical that you continue to assess whether it is living up to expectations. Is it meeting the goals it set for itself? Is it continuing to announce plans for new products in the future? If the answer to one or both of these questions is no, it's probably time to swallow your pride, admit you were wrong, and let that stock go.

Perhaps your thesis is predicated on the idea that a company will successfully engage in mergers and acquisitions to maintain a competitive edge. If your investment thesis involves this sort of strategy, analyze a company's recent M&A to see whether it's been successful. Have the acquisitions generally been accretive to the bottom line? Has the company seen improved competitiveness or revenue diversification as a result? If not, the company may be allocating inefficiently, squandering resources, and missing opportunities.

These examples highlight that being "first and alone" is a major advantage for any company. You may be rewarded handsomely if you can find one of these companies early on. Remember, though, that nothing lasts forever. Be careful about companies that become complacent with their market dominance, and be wary of new entrants in a space that can disrupt the market and dislodge the current leader (and your portfolio, as a result).

CONTINUOUS LEARNING REQUIRES SORTING

What has always appealed to me about the investment process is that I had to learn continuously to do it well. As a result, I wake up every day trying to learn as much as possible. I feel that it's imperative for me to know everything going on in the world, how it might impact the financial markets, and, in certain instances, how it will impact my investment thesis and my portfolios.

So I read the *Wall Street Journal* and the *New York Times* thoroughly. I try not to watch much television, only because on television, I'm subject to what the producers of the content want to put in front of me rather than what I need to know. In a newspaper, if an article covers something that will not help me learn, I can move on; I don't have that option on television.

Learning continuously also means adapting to changing life circumstances and compromising with the people in your life whom your decisions will impact. A few years ago, I was looking over my personal investment portfolio and happened to leave the statements from Morgan Stanley on the table. Glancing at them, Anita turned to me and asked, "Do you know how old you are?" I assured her that I knew very well how old I was, to which she responded, "This looks like the portfolio of a twenty-three-year-old, not an eighty-year-old!"

She asked me to do her and myself a favor and take enough money out of the portfolio to live on for the rest of our lives, at our current quality of life, and put it in Treasury bills or some other secure short-term instruments. If I did that, she said she would never bother me about being too speculative in my portfolio again. I like being at risk, and I like investing in growth companies. That's what excites me. But it's also important to acknowledge the importance of shifting your portfolio as circumstances in your life change.

Continuous learning can be difficult when it feels impossible to know what is important. This problem has only gotten harder with time.

SORTING THROUGH
INFORMATION OVERLOAD

Toward the beginning of my career, in the summer of 1966, I was invited to give a talk in Lima, Peru, by a classmate of mine from HBS who was a professor there. His name was C L Kendall (we never did find out what the unpunctuated initials stood for). The talk I gave was on the topic of "too much information." I had brought a stack of research to read during my travels. I told the audience, "I get so much information, I don't even have time to sort it."

That was the dilemma I faced more than fifty years ago. Now the problem is much worse. Not only do we have all the printed reports from various brokerage firms and other traditional forms of research, but we also have vast amounts of information available on the internet. The various mediums by which this knowledge is disseminated have also proliferated.

Sorting is the path to success in most intellectual pursuits.

Spending your time on what has practical utility is imperative. In the case of strategy, I find three or four sources of information useful, and while I occasionally read something by somebody else, I focus most of my time on my own thinking. And that could be said for individual sector research. It is also possible to underestimate the value of the newspaper. Every day, I learn something from the *Wall Street Journal* and the *New York Times* and, on the weekends, *Barron's*.

When you're starting out, it can be overwhelming to parse the information thrown at you. That's an important reason to find mentors who will help you. You can also find yourself being asked questions you don't have answers to and must research to find. The combination of mentorship and external pressures to find answers to tough questions will enable you to find what you need. You can explore more creative sources in your own time and develop your own system of what works as a regular source of information for your function.

I pay attention to a couple of economic research firms, a couple of technical firms, a few blogs, and the daily newspapers. Occasionally,

I'll read something from another source if the title or subject catches my eye. But I try to whittle down the number of inputs, and my decision-making has improved. I have become more disciplined in my approach and rely more on my own judgment than my *interpretation* of the judgment of others.

There have been various efforts throughout the years to restrict the payment for research by brokerage firms. For example, when the rules were changed such that people were required to pay cash to brokerage firms for their research, it was expected to reduce the amount of research produced. Interestingly, the opposite has occurred, even though brokerage firms complain about insufficient money to produce research. One effect has been that the compensation provided to research analysts, which used to range up to millions of dollars per year, has fallen significantly over the past several decades. I suspect that this can only hurt the quality of the output that is created over time.

UTILIZING OUTSIDE MANAGERS

I also use outside managers like hedge funds, managed by people with as much talent (or more than) I have. There are a number of them out there, and they change. Typically, people are best at this when they are under fifty years old. When you get older, you get set in your ways and less resilient than you should be to adapting to a continuously changing environment. I have residual holdings in some of the managers to whom I originally allocated.

Hedge fund managers generally tend to be of a few types, following certain investment philosophies, such as value, growth, and quantitative. The good ones make enough money that, at some point, they give up managing other people's money and focus on managing their own. Lee Cooperman at Omega is an example of that. Sometimes, when I invest with somebody, I don't have to take my money out; they give it back. But other managers could go on forever, and firms like Viking, run by Andreas Halvorsen, can go on and do a good job.

The good thing there is that you get the value of compounding. They take profits during the year, but the firm's base tends to be buy-and-hold. I have money with both kinds: people who terminate and people who are sustainable. About half my money is managed by outside managers, and the other half is managed by myself. I view that as an important form of diversification because all my personally managed money is invested in growth areas.

One of the great things about the US tax law is that capital appreciation is untaxed until the stock is sold. If I followed this policy, I would have a portfolio continuously appreciating in value and being untaxed. The stock market rises three-quarters of the time. Bear markets only occupy one-quarter of the time. So over a long period of time, the portfolio will have a great opportunity to grow in value. And that's the way it worked out. I chose most of the good stocks that I picked in the 1970s and 1980s; in many cases, I have made ten times my initial investment or even more.

Now that we have discussed some of the traits of successful investors, we can discuss some of the key things I look for in a successful investment.

STRONG PROFIT MARGINS

I've found these successful qualities boil down to margins and innovation. You don't need to be a professional investor to understand what makes a good company. All sorts of life experiences have taught me the importance of certain elements of an attractive investment opportunity. The same is probably true for you, whether you know it or not.

For example, when I worked for the Brass Rail Restaurants, I gained a very clear understanding of profit margins. The restaurant business must be one of the worst businesses in the world. Think about it as a manufacturing plant in a high-rent location, with perishable raw materials (and finished goods), unable to derive revenue on rainy, snowy days or holidays, where the lowest-level employee interfaces with your customer, and where the competition is usually intense. Supermarkets suffer from similar dynamics.

It's no wonder that margins in the restaurant and supermarket business are very low (except for very popular, high-end ones), and it's also no wonder many go out of business. Even if you have a popular restaurant, it only seems so for a reasonable period, until the public decides to gravitate somewhere else. Manufacturing, too, often has low profit margins, especially in producing goods with expensive raw materials with frequent and significant price fluctuations.

Service businesses of certain kinds can do very well—investment management and private equity, for example—and often have good margins. In a business where you charge by the hour, like a law firm, it's very hard to have a high profit ratio. The people doing the work want a high proportion of their revenue.

I've tried focusing on places with high profit margins when looking for investments. What are some examples? These are in extractive industries, like oil and mining, financial services, asset management, and pharmaceuticals, where developing an important drug with significant healing powers can command a high price.

Think about the money management industry. You are paid for being the commander of the capital. Before 1980, money management firms did very well for years with a fee of half a percent or a full percent. Those were considered good fees. After the advent of the hedge fund, fees of 1 to 1.5 percent of management fees and 20 percent of profits became more common, and it was possible for a money manager who was doing very well to become very rich at a relatively young age.

Think about it—if you can raise a one-billion-dollar fund, you will generate $10 million to $20 million in management fees alone every year. Hiring a couple of staff and renting office space in Midtown Manhattan would cost less than a million dollars per year. In addition to that, you get 20 percent of the profits. If you can appreciate the $1 billion by 20 percent, that's another $200 million, and you get $40 million. Not to mention that you are now receiving management fees on a higher base. So getting very rich at a young age is possible if you are a good stock-picker.

Similarly, developing a drug in the pharmaceutical industry is very expensive. But if you do develop an important treatment for a widespread disease, the profits can be considerable. The same is true in technology. So many of my most favorable investments have been in technology, biotechnology, energy, and financial services.

I have always thought that high profit margins have another advantage—in adversity, you can still make money, even though your margin may shrink. Traditional industrial companies, conversely, may suffer outright negative earnings during a recession. So I advise that one of the first things you look at when analyzing a company is to consider the profit margins, whether they've been sustainable or improving, and whether they are resilient to downturns. As a rule of thumb, I like to see pretax margins of 30 percent or more before I consider investing.

CONSISTENT INNOVATION

The key is the ability to maintain a good profit margin, and that's where innovation comes in. As discussed earlier, an important element of avoiding thesis creep is to ensure that a company continues to innovate consistently.

First, some cautionary tales. When I first entered the financial services business, the money management firm I worked at had heavy investments in Xerox and Polaroid. The original Xerox copying machine (the 914 plain paper copier) was being bought by every business you could imagine. Everybody had to have one, and when the smaller product (the 813 copier) came into being, that also met great popularity. The Polaroid camera had characteristics that made it attractive to all kinds of people—from tourists to Andy Warhol.

Over time, both the Xerox and the Polaroid products were displaced. Other people developed copying machines to compete with Xerox, and the company subsequently diversified itself into other businesses, including financial services. In the case of Polaroid, cameras were replaced by people taking pictures on their phones. As fate would have it, the Polaroid is now experiencing a resurgence among younger people who find novelty in old-fashioned-looking pictures or the ability to take photos without being tethered to their phones. It is unlikely to ever retain any significant market share in picture-taking, however, and Eastman Kodak is out of the photography business now.

Businesses with a stronghold on a particular market must be examined because they can be displaced. When you hold stock in a company with a favorable profit margin, you must always look for competition because a high profit margin is attractive to competitors. Suppose they can replicate a product without violating a patent or develop a different product with the same application that can be a substitute. In that case, you can find yourself out of business rather than enjoying the profit margin you have now. So while I have advocated "buy and hold" strategies, I am vigilant about changes, and I have found several stocks that stood the test of time. However, in many cases, the peak prices on the NYSE or the OTC market were behind them. The peak price occurred when the product was very much in favor, and the competition was nowhere in sight.

The question is, Does that apply to companies like Apple, Amazon, Google, and Facebook? We know it applies to Netflix because competition is an apparent problem there. But does it apply to those former four heavyweights? There is a concept of being "first and alone"—at HBS, they teach that if you're an entrepreneur, you should try to get big fast to discourage competition. There have been other search engines like Google, but they have not been able to acquire a dominant place in the market to topple Google from the top of the pedestal. For now, Facebook has maintained its position as the preeminent social media entity. It would be subject to competition as a retailer, but they're so big and so much of a household word that they look pretty secure to me.

Look back at the Nifty Fifty. Many of those stocks, including Polaroid, Xerox, Avon, Eastman Kodak, Sears Roebuck, and others, are no longer competitive. So there is a possibility that the FAANG stocks eventually fall to competitors. But an example is that Microsoft has been around for some time, and no one has yet been able to displace it as the primary software service. It remains a formidable software empire.

The managers of these very successful businesses are very aware of the competitive threat. Their large profit margins enable them to engage in research and development projects to develop the next new "thing" that can be the engine of growth for its business and ward off competition. That's another advantage of having a high profit margin and being "first and alone," and we know this has been the case for Google, Facebook, and Amazon. I once spent a day with a group in New York called "Google Ideas," run by a bright young man whose job was to come up with product or service ideas that didn't exist but might have appeal in the market. He had a team of scruffy-looking young people working there who could bring their dogs to the office (and which were running all over the place), but all this bright young man cared about was hiring creative people. He didn't care where—or if—they went to college; he was only concerned with whether they had fresh ideas. I think you will see more of that, as we already see in Silicon Valley in a large dimension in the tech company "incubators."

You could argue that the industries I've identified are taking advantage of innocent customers, either people vulnerable to a disease or people who have money to invest but are too naive to do so. The prices are determined by the efficacy of the products or what the market will bear. In the case of pharmaceuticals, the company is trying to get a reasonable return on the speculative investment they have made in the product to get it developed, approved, and brought to market. I don't view that as a predatory practice. Some of these fee structures or profit margins develop over time, and a newcomer to the business just follows the historical practice. But it does result in the ability of the practitioners to make a lot of money in a very short time if they are successful in identifying something—whether a natural resource reserve, a pharmaceutical product, or an approach to the financial markets that are in favor.

A good rule of thumb regarding valuations is that the multiple should be parallel to the growth rate. By that, I mean the stock is getting overpriced when a company's multiple (such as its price-to-earnings ratio) exceeds its earnings growth rate. In addition to that, you've got to watch the competitive environment. Eastman Kodak maintained a high multiple when photography was dependent on traditional methods. But when photography became digital, taking pictures with film essentially became obsolete, save for only the most hard-core of old-school picture-takers. A good example of this dynamic today is Netflix, which once dominated the industry but now faces stiff competition. We've seen that play out in recent earnings, and the company's stock price plummeted.

Also, dividends are an alternative approach. Companies with good and increasing dividends can be attractive too. They tend to be something other than growth companies. Some of them are in businesses with an important market share that they can maintain for long periods. In the case of some private equity companies, they have generous and increasing dividends and earnings growth, so you can access both investment strategies simultaneously.

A strong investment philosophy balances thorough research with decisive action, a long-term perspective, and regular reassessment of your investment theses. Successful investors blend conviction with adaptability, ensuring decisions are based on solid fundamentals while staying flexible in changing circumstances. As you refine your investment compass, remember that diligence, discipline, and a willingness to learn are key. Whether you prefer value or growth investing, let your passion for discovery guide you, and stay true to your principles. This approach will help you achieve lasting success in the dynamic investing world.

CHAPTER 6

NEVER RETIRE

Never retire. If you work forever, you can live forever. I know there is an abundance of biological evidence against this theory, but I'm going with it anyway.

While I was still at Morgan Stanley, I was interviewed by a reporter from the *New York Times*. It was during the late summer in East Hampton. We sat outside, the sun shining as we looked over Georgica Pond. During the interview, he asked me, "Why do you keep doing it? Haven't you made enough money? Why don't you stay out here, go to the beach, and relax for the rest of your life?"

I told him I do it because I like to be a part of what's happening. I want to interpret the reality I see before me and find it very stimulating. My job is to forecast the future, and no one can do that, but I give it my best effort, and occasionally, I get things right. I synthesize all the variables influencing the financial markets, how they will have an impact, and what I see before me turns out to be a new reality.

"It's a big thrill when I get it right," I told him. The reporter looked at me quizzically and asked, "How big a thrill can that be, really?" I looked at him and said, "It's better than sex." He thought for a moment before replying, "Maybe for you."

CHOOSE ENJOYMENT OVER COMPENSATION

My sixteenth Life Lesson goes as follows:

> When seeking a career as you come out of school or making a job change, always take the job that looks like it will be the most enjoyable. If it pays the most, you're lucky. If it doesn't, take it anyway. I took a severe pay cut to accept each of the two best jobs I've ever had, and they both turned out to be exceptionally rewarding financially.

I've had five important jobs in my career. I took two for money, and they both turned out to be mistakes. I took pay cuts in the other three jobs—in my first role on Wall Street, at Morgan Stanley, and at Blackstone—and these were the ones that turned out to be the most consequential in my life. I have advised young people who were considering taking jobs they didn't think they would enjoy just for $5,000 bonuses. My advice to them, as it is to anyone in a similar situation, is not to be afraid to take a job that pays less or even take a pay cut to pursue a job that they think they would love and that is tailored to leverage their strengths.

Remember, there is a perfect job out there for everyone. So keep looking if you don't think you have it yet. Always take a job that provides work you are going to love. In other words—and this is related to the lesson above—the work content is more important than the compensation. You will spend many hours at this job, and you should look forward to throwing yourself into it, not to the money you will get from it. If you must spend eight to twelve hours per day (more if you're in banking or private equity) doing work you don't like, it will be torturous. I've made much more money than I ever expected I would. The only explanation I can think of is that I was doing what I loved and was successful professionally and financially as a result.

CAREER TRANSITIONS AND LESSONS LEARNED

While you may never plan to retire, you must adapt to changing circumstances. "Don't retire" should not be understood to mean "Become a crusty relic resistant to change."

One important thing to do is to replace yourself. In 2000, I was sixty-seven years old, and while I was not interested in retiring, I began to think that I couldn't be the number-one strategist at Morgan Stanley forever. Barton Biggs had left the firm around this time to start a hedge fund because the trading restrictions at Morgan Stanley were hampering his ability to manage his own money. The combination of those events caused me to go to the firm and tell them we should find someone who could be my successor. We hired a headhunter, and the names they came up with included Steven Galbraith. Steve had been a financial service analyst and a partner at Sanford C. Bernstein, and his work was terrific. I thought he could do the job as well as I did and maybe better.

Steve joined the firm in 2001 and eventually succeeded me as chief US strategist, at which time I became senior US strategist. Soon, his work became better accepted than mine, and he became the top-ranked investment strategist on Wall Street in the Institutional Investor research poll. He had a brilliant career with the firm until he left to join

Maverick Capital in 2004. As a result, I was again the head US strategist at Morgan Stanley. I was sorry to see Steve go, but he felt he could make some serious money at Maverick, and he eventually started his own firm, just as Barton did. He eventually closed it and now manages money with his wife, who had also worked at Morgan Stanley.

Leadership changes can also throw you for a loop. I encountered the most intriguing leadership episode of my professional career during these years at Morgan Stanley. The issue was between Phil Purcell, who had been the chief executive of Dean Witter, and John Mack, who had been the chief executive of Morgan Stanley, at the time of the two companies' merger in 1997. The two could not have been more opposite in nature.

Phil Purcell was a McKinsey-trained Australian who was absorbed in strategy and planning. He was not a "people person" and surrounded himself with people who generally agreed with him and thought him to be the smartest person in any room he entered. John Mack was more of a people person and more intuitive in his approach. He recognized the need for planning in a big organization but was willing to make decisions based on the circumstances as they developed.

As I understood it, the original agreement was for Purcell to be chairman of the combined firm for four years and Mack to be the chairman after that. The working relationship between the two men did not go well. It was a clash of personalities more than anything else: the McKinsey technocrat and the Morgan Stanley basketball coach. The struggle led Mack to leave the firm in 2001, taking on the role of CEO of Credit Suisse First Boston shortly thereafter. However, the tension between Purcell and Mack had already damaged the morale of Morgan Stanley's employees, such that a group of eight former managing directors at Morgan Stanley banded together to suggest that Purcell step down, which he finally did in June 2005.

One important lesson is that chief executives can be planners and strategists but must also be oriented toward working with people. Their job is to be coaches who can draw the most out of their team, not to micromanage or attempt to do all the work themselves. There will always be a certain number of ceremonial and procedural tasks that a chief executive must do, like dealing with the board and direct reports.

But the major job of a company leader is to hire the best people, motivate them to do the job effectively, and monitor their performance. If you are interested in pursuing a leadership role of this nature, consider whether you have the necessary skills. If you don't naturally possess them, work on improving them.

Other than the leadership lessons I took from this experience, the circumstance had personal relevance for my career and my plans never to retire. In the spring of 2005, shortly before Purcell stepped down, I was approached by Art Samberg, whom I had worked with at Weiss, Peck & Greer, and John Mack, who by this time had left Credit Suisse and was now a free agent. Samberg and Mack came to me and said that the latter was planning to join Pequot Capital, Samberg's very successful money management firm, and that they wanted me to join too.

I developed a very close relationship with Mack during the time that we overlapped at Morgan Stanley, and Samberg and I maintained a strong personal and professional friendship after I left Weiss, Peck & Greer. They told me they thought we could build a great firm together. I tentatively accepted their offer. In 2005, I had been at Morgan Stanley for twenty-one years, and I felt it might be time to do something else. I could make a lot of money as part of a hedge fund. I was financially independent by that time, but I could use the additional funds to contribute to charity.

But there was a twist. After Purcell left Morgan Stanley, the firm immediately approached John Mack to become CEO. Mack had always wanted that job, and with Purcell out of the picture, his vindication had finally arrived. He accepted the position at Morgan Stanley and subsequently withdrew from the Pequot partnership, which left me hanging. I went to Mack and asked him what I should do, and he—I think feeling guilty for disappointing Art Samberg—encouraged me to join Pequot anyway. I did so in 2005 and remained at the firm for four years.

In 2009, an insider trading case, which had previously been put to bed by the Securities and Exchange Commission, resurrected itself. It involved an incident in 2001 before I got to Pequot, but the case alleged that Art Samberg had been caught up in a possible insider trading transgression. In May 2009, Art decided to close the firm because of this incident that had taken place eight years earlier. The case would be in the press, and he thought, correctly, that it would be impossible to raise money in such an environment. The firm was to be shuttered in August 2009, and he informed all the employees, including me.

I didn't want to retire, but here I was out on the street at seventy-six years old, and I didn't think anyone would want to hire me.

Turns out I was wrong. Twenty-four different firms contacted me, and I agreed to conversations with about a dozen of them. These included Chilton Investment, where I was very friendly with Richard Chilton, and Zweig-DiMenna, as I had become friends with Joe DiMenna.

Then Tom Hill, who was head of Blackstone Alternative Asset Management, called me up and asked me what I would do with the rest of my life. I told him that I wanted to continue to work and didn't intend to retire. He told me they had been looking for a strategist for two years and wanted me to talk with them. I had an appointment with Tony James, and he set up meetings with fifteen other people at Blackstone, including Jon Gray, Prakash Melwani, and Steve Schwarzman, whom I knew well from playing tennis with him in the 1980s.

FIND THE RIGHT PLATFORM AND TEAM

Finding the right platform for your work and being on a team that is a good fit for you are important elements of staying powerful in your career.

In my latest career transition, it was clear from the beginning that Blackstone was the right platform. It was a much smaller firm back then, with around $100 billion in assets under management and around twelve hundred employees. Of all the firms I was considering joining, Blackstone was the "riskiest" in terms of my career because it had a pioneering role.

They had never had a strategist before, and I would need to prove my value in what felt like a vacuum. They had operated successfully up to that point without a strategist, and it would be up to me to prove that they could operate more effectively with one. I started by attending the weekly Monday morning meeting. I thought the meeting would benefit from a macro outlook, and I told the organizers that I should have a five-minute segment to talk about the macro environment in which the firm and our investors operate. It became a recurring segment. This weekly meeting has evolved over the years into a high-powered production called *Blackstone TV*—and I speak now about once a month amid a rotating cast of other speakers.

When deciding, I was most interested in working in the job that would make me happiest, and I thought that Blackstone would do that in the final stage of my career. Looking back, I realize I made the right decision. I already had enough net worth for any charitable contributions I wanted to make, in addition to benefiting my family. Still, my priority was doing what I loved, and I've been able to do that at Blackstone.

Attitude is the most important characteristic in selecting people to work with you. Try to pick somebody who is eager to take on the job, whether that role be a personal assistant or an analyst. If they love the job, they will throw themselves into it with an enthusiasm that will be indispensable to their own success and that of the broader team.

Once I had a personal assistant who had all the skills she needed for the job but had several personal problems that detracted from her effectiveness. While it's always important to help the people who work for you where you can, there will be limits to what you can do. In this case, she was unable to manage her personal problems effectively, and there was nothing I could do to completely alleviate them. It's important to work with people who are interested in supporting you and feel personal fulfillment when they do.

Pick the smartest person you can find because, in addition to attitude, intelligence is a critical characteristic to have. Hopefully, the person will be even smarter than you, which will upgrade your performance. Also, think about the needs of the broader team—at Blackstone, we now have a team of Taylor Becker, Joe Zidle, and me, and we work very well together.

My executive assistant, Maria, has been working with me for fourteen years. She is a big part of our team and supports all of us.

I doubt there is any other personal assistant who would take on as much responsibility as she does, yet she does excellent work and never complains.

I mention all this to highlight the fact that all our team members like each other, we all feel we can benefit from one another's creativity, and we turn out a terrific product and have been doing so for the last several years. The way our team works together and the lack of friction or personal animosity are real assets. This is generally true of the nature of Blackstone as a firm, and I think that's why the firm is so successful.

It was not necessarily evident that I would start another chapter in my professional career after my time at Pequot ended. Still, retirement was not an attractive option for me, because I like working. I like interacting with others and having a purpose when I wake up every day. I like being with clients and learning from them. I like the challenge of trying to develop a useful investment strategy. I didn't have my fill of it after around thirty years in the industry, and I don't think I ever will.

While I've been risk averse in my career, I haven't been so in my investments. I understand the stock market better than my career path and probably have more confidence in my ability to invest than in my ability to advance my career. If I make a mistake in a stock, I can always sell it. If I make a mistake in a job choice, I can't just quit it at will. Taking a job implies a certain commitment, and I can only make that commitment so many times in a given career.

Millennials have a different attitude about this, but as you grow older, you don't have the same flexibility to make career changes as you do in your twenties and thirties. Making wholesale career changes in your fifties or sixties is much harder. In other words, when I went from Morgan Stanley to Pequot, that was only because Pequot reached out to me. When I was seventy-six years old, and Pequot closed, I didn't think I would get any job offers, and it was to my pleasant surprise that people did contact me—and only because, by that time, I had established a platform and reputation that could prove useful in a marketing sense.

Certainly, that's what Chilton saw and what Blackstone saw, among others. They thought I could bring my personal brand to the firm and help them build a business. If you haven't established a brand or reputation for accomplishing something by the time you're in your fifties, changing jobs is very hard. As a portfolio manager, you must have an excellent record to change jobs in the second half of your first century.

When I was thinking about my career, I thought I would be most comfortable working in a small firm. I thought the nature of my personality and my need for individualism wouldn't work well in a big company. That was a big mistake. I worked in small firms until I got to Morgan Stanley in 1985 and was successful in those jobs. But when I got to Morgan Stanley and had a big platform to operate from, I began to thrive.

I made several observations from this experience. One, when you work at a large place, you interact with the people immediately around you on your team, but you don't interact with the entire firm all that much. So even with an abrasive personality, you can't rub too many people in a big firm the wrong way. You can do that with your close associates, but you learn how to adapt to them, and vice versa.

The other observation I made was that when I was at Morgan Stanley, I had an expansive platform. I was chief US strategist, and when I wrote things, suddenly, there would be coverage in large newspapers like the *Wall Street Journal* and the *New York Times*, and I was also on TV news with increasing frequency. This made it easier for me to meet people and build my network. So I found I did well in a large firm. When I left Morgan Stanley and then after I left my subsequent job at Pequot, I had multiple offers, but Blackstone was the only offer that would allow me to operate on a large platform. By then, I had learned that a big firm suited my personality and abilities better than a small firm.

This speaks to an important lesson. You need to react to your environment earlier in your career. Do you prefer large groups or working with only one or two people? I found that I like working in environments with a lot of people around me, even though I may only play a small role in the grand scheme of things.

For example, I recently had a visit from Mike Casey, who used to be a lead marketer in Blackstone's real estate group. He came to me to discuss his career and to get my view of the economic outlook. The fact that I've made friends throughout the firm and maintain them even after they leave is satisfying. I like to think that when I come to work every day, I work with friends. And I look forward to being with them.

The issue post-COVID-19 has been working remotely, and I don't have the interpersonal interaction that provided so much satisfaction to me. I am a people person; I like working with groups and interacting with them, even if many disagree. I like defending my positions. Yet I want to work in an atmosphere that encourages me to be original, come up with my own ideas, and be constructive in sharing those ideas with others.

Blackstone has been a perfect example of that. It's the best place I've ever worked. Some of the distinguishing features of the firm are that it encourages people to take risks and that the safety net is close to where you're jumping, so if you fall, they'll catch you. Because they excel by being more creative than other firms, taking risks is part of our DNA and has led to continual expansion.

In the investment strategy group, we are encouraged to think creatively about the outlook, recognizing that if we have an idea that significantly differs from the consensus, we run the risk of being wrong. This is part of what has made the firm so successful. It's this commitment to creativity and intellectual honesty that is one of the reasons the firm has become the largest alternative investment manager in the world and continues to enjoy success.

CHAPTER 7

BUILDING A LEGACY

In this book, I have shared my reflections on my Twenty Life Lessons. Most, if not all, of these lessons are valuable for everyone, regardless of where they are in their own journey.

During your early years, it is crucial to focus on improving your skills and constantly strive to become a better version of yourself. This requires concentrated, inward focus and dedication to figure out your talents and what you might set out to do and succeed in. I would be hard-pressed to say that I have not done everything in my power to become the best version of myself. I may not have done so perfectly, but I have achieved more success than I ever hoped for.

Now that I'm a decade shy of a century, I want to introduce a new, previously unannounced life lesson for those in the later stages of your journey. This twenty-first Life Lesson is:

> Turn your focus outward. Once you have ascended to the top rung of your respective ladder, it's incumbent upon you to turn around and extend a hand to help others climb up and do the same.

This is the topic of the final chapter of this book, and I am practicing it as I enter my fourth thirty-year span. There are several ways to do this, and I'll share several here, including the importance of mentoring, recognizing others, and thinking about giving back.

MENTORSHIP

If you've achieved great success in life, don't hoard the knowledge you've gathered for yourself. Share it with others. As I've discussed, the investment world grows more complex and challenging each decade. I daresay it's true in nearly every industry. Help the emerging class in whatever industry you call yours. It will multiply your impact, and it will leave you deeply satisfied. It helps you answer the question of "So now what?" once you have reached the pinnacle of your chosen vocation. My eighteenth Life Lesson says:

> When your children are grown or if you have no children, always find someone younger to mentor. It is very satisfying to help someone steer through life's obstacles, and you'll be surprised at how much you will learn in the process.

I've mentored dozens of people during my long career. More, perhaps, than even I know. I hope I've been helpful to those people, and I know I've derived a lot of personal joy from it. I've learned a lot from my mentees. Many of them are much smarter than I am, and they only lack experience. While I have a reasonable amount of intelligence, I have a large amount of experience, and I can share that with others.

I've been able to help a number of my mentees at crucial junctures in their lives, such as when they are building a family or changing jobs. Some of them have become dependent on me for help. To be a good mentor, you must understand the person you're mentoring.

Every person is different and requires different skills for good mentorship. There's no one-size-fits-all.

Some people are highly intelligent but emotionally immature and tend to make ineffective decisions. Some people are street smart but less book smart. Some people have aspirations well beyond their abilities, and I've found that most people are immobile—they should be changing jobs or making other life changes when they are at a dead end, but they are just too comfortable to do so.

Recognizing the person's nature in relation to their circumstance is the mentor's job. I've learned a lot of technology skills from my mentees and have been useful to them in providing career guidance. In some cases, providing family guidance has been helpful too—regarding having children, how many to have—and whether someone should get married or divorced. But the key to it is to apply your personal experience to the predicament of the mentee. You can't do that effectively without understanding the person thoroughly. That requires spending time with him or her.

In some cases, I've been explicitly sought out for a mentorship role. It's flattering, but it can also prove to be very useful. I am the godfather to multiple kids, including a handful who have asked me themselves to do so. It can work out quite well when you are hand-picked by the person who will benefit from your mentorship. Because the person is open to you, there is something you have done to impress them or otherwise make them think favorably of you, and they are open to your suggestions. When you fall into or are forced into a mentorship position, the person may not be as receptive.

I try never to say no, but it is sometimes inevitable. Sometimes, the logistics of the situation won't work out. Other times, I don't know the person well enough and don't have the inclination to invest the time required to forge a strong personal connection. Once in a while, you get a real star as a mentee. I've had a few, and I take great pride in watching them soar beyond me. You don't ask for any compensation or recognition for it. It is joy enough to watch that person succeed and develop—whether professionally or personally—and share in that success.

You must only mentor someone if you will find personal fulfillment solely based on their growth and development. Never expect anything material in return. That's not a noble purpose. Do it for the joy of watching that person become even more successful than you have been, and if you pick the right mentees, that can happen—and more than once.

RECOGNIZING OTHERS

A related concept to mentorship is recognizing others, which is the eleventh Life Lesson.

> Take the time to give those who work for you a pat on the back when they do good work. Most people are so focused on the next challenge that they fail to thank the people who support them. It is important to do this. It motivates and inspires people and encourages them to perform at a higher level.

It is imperative to motivate your team. People who work with me know they can come into my office whenever they want and ask me anything. There is no work so important that I can't return to it after being distracted. Part of being a leader is to be a mentor, but it's also important to be a motivator. Helping people become as effective as they can be is something I take very seriously.

I became very interested in Morgan Stanley's history during my time there. A partner named Fred Whittemore was generally understood to be the keeper of the firm's culture. He would often address new employees on the topic. I felt he romanticized the firm's history, talking only about the good and never about its failings.

One day, I told him that I wanted to be the "apprentice culture carrier." It turned out that around the same time, an author named Ron Chernow had published a book called *The House of Morgan*. The book detailed the firm's history, but Chernow did not have the cooperation of Morgan Stanley when he wrote it. Until publishing this book, he had been a journalist at *Mother Jones*, and the powers at Morgan Stanley felt that his credentials did not merit writing a book about the vaunted firm. He did so anyway, without their input.

I contacted Chernow, informing him that I intended to become the culture carrier of the company. Having read his book thoroughly, I wanted to meet him, and we had several conversations. Finally, I arranged to have him speak at Morgan Stanley's annual conference for investors at Lyford Cay, which was a real breakthrough. He did a great job and impressed the top executives of the firm. We became close personal friends over the years, and he spoke at my eighty-fifth birthday party. I have also helped him with financial advice along the way. As the historical consultant for the hit Broadway show *Hamilton*, he gets a royalty from the musical's productions. He has gone from modest living to a wealthier position, and I could not feel better about it.

"THE SMARTEST MAN IN EUROPE"

Of course, in your own life, you should also seek out mentors, as I did with the man I called the "Smartest Man in Europe."

During the '80s and '90s, Morgan Stanley held an annual conference for portfolio managers at Lyford Cay in the Bahamas. Leading hedge fund managers like Andreas Halvorsen, Julian Robertson, George Soros, and others attended. We also had some people come from Europe, like Edgar de Picciotto and Niels Taub. The relationships I developed with these people during that period proved very valuable to me later on. In particular, I formed an important friendship with Edgar de Picciotto.

Edgar was an exotic figure whose ancestors operated canteens along the Silk Road between the Middle East and China. He had entered the financial business and married a woman whose father was the chairman of the Trade Development Bank, which was eventually sold to American Express. He later started his private bank in Geneva, Union Bancaire Privée. He could see events developing long before they did. He was the first person I knew of who saw Japan's investment potential. He anticipated the fall of the Berlin Wall and the collapse of the Soviet Union.

Of all the people attending the Lyford Cay conferences, he was the one I thought I could learn the most from. I started out by having dinner or lunch with him whenever I had a business trip to Geneva. One time, I got the idea of writing him up as the "Smartest Man in Europe." I had no idea whether he was actually the smartest man on the continent, but it seemed like a good label to assign him. I wrote the first essay about him in 2001 and continued to do so every year until he passed away in 2016.

In addition to the annual meeting in Lyford Cay, he had a summer home in Saint-Jean-Cap-Ferrat in southern France, where my wife and I would spend several days in the early summer. It was one of only private residences designed by Oscar Niemeyer, the architect of Brasilia. Niemeyer had designed mainly commercial buildings, but he did Edgar's residence. It was in shambles when he started, but he restored it beautifully. The home even included one of the famous Jeff Koons balloon dogs at the entrance; it was fuchsia and twenty-five feet tall, having to be brought in by crane. On those days that I would visit him, we would spend three days talking about the world, the market, personal philosophy, investing, and everything else.

Until I met Edgar, I thought having a diversified investment portfolio made the most sense. One of the things I learned from him is that there are only a few good ideas at a given point in time, so one should try to identify them and own those and not the other stuff. When the investments become mature or obsolete, one should sell them and go on to something else. That was his investment philosophy, and I adopted parts of it for myself. In his view, diversification only diluted the great ideas.

He encouraged me to network as broadly as possible, as he did himself. Every year when we came to Geneva, he would throw a dinner with Stephen Roach and me, and he would invite the investment leaders of the community to meet with us. So he used entertainment as a networking device, and he was part of the inspiration for my own Benchmark Lunches.

For all the years I wrote the Smartest Man essays, people wanted to know who the subject was, and out of respect for his privacy, I never revealed his identity (while he was alive). Everyone looked forward to reading these essays about him like they did the Ten Surprises. People responded well to the series because I was revealing the thinking of a certified billionaire who had made his money primarily through investing; it became a template for the right investment posture at that point in time.

We never discussed whether I would reveal his identity, but I decided not to. I thought if I had revealed it, people would call him up and bother him. Thus, I thought it was important not to reveal his identity. Why would he let me write this essay and share all his state secrets? I think he got some satisfaction out of reading these and thinking that thousands of people read them too. He didn't suffer for it, and the few people who found out who he was complimented him for it. So he got the exposure he wanted without the intrusions he abhorred.

Edgar became an important figure in my life and a mentor. After he passed away, I wrote a requiem in his honor. In my final "Smartest Man" essay, I recalled all the things I had learned from him over the years. Here is a short excerpt of my reflections on our relationship (the full essay is included in the appendix):

Over the years I've learned that mentors fall into two categories. There are those you work with every day who are continuously guiding you to improved performance. The late Barton Biggs, my colleague at Morgan Stanley, falls into that category. He developed the concept of "impressionistic strategy," writing his essays in the first person as though he was in a conversation with investors rather than in a totally objective style similar to an academic paper. He was totally devoted to his work, and he never wasted time. He would take an hour out of each day to exercise, and he loved sports like tennis, golf and touch football, but when he wasn't exercising, he was reading and writing, and his output included essays and two books with a third in process when he passed away.

The second type of mentor is one whom you see intermittently. These individuals provide guidance because of who they are and what they do. Edgar fell into that category, and I am forever grateful to him for what he taught me. He was fond of breaking rules.

Suspicious of diversification as the hiding ground for those without conviction, he believed in concentration: If he liked a country, a sector, or an asset class, he was willing to put considerable money into it and exclude representation in other areas more popular with institutional investors. He sought high rewards and was willing to tolerate high risk in the process, once buying an office building in Iraq and selling it a short time later after it had doubled. He was not a trader, but he knew that a good investment had three phases: the period when you are waiting for an offbeat, but promising, idea to work; the period when everyone agrees with you, and the stock or asset performs well; and the final period when the asset may still be appreciating, but it is time to look for something else because the additional gains will be small. It can be dangerous to overstay a position. I still have not learned this lesson. He was particularly skillful at selling his mistakes quickly. Happily, I have learned that lesson.

He taught me the value of trust and the joy of friendship and the futility of envy. He was proud of his own success but also an admirer of the success of others who were his friends. He never talked about missed opportunities except when he was criticizing himself. He was his own toughest critic and he encouraged me to be the same. Even if you are an intelligent risk taker, you will make many mistakes. Recognize them early, but never stop taking risks, because that is where the real opportunities are, and your life will be more stimulating as a result.

GIVING BACK

An interesting thing happens when you officially become "old." By that, I don't just mean the aches, pains, gray hairs, or missing hairs accompanying aging. I mean that stage of your life where just about anyone, including your elders, would describe you as a senior citizen. It's a little rude, but it's also fair. It's also sobering because it forces you to look back upon your life and try to figure out what's become of you—what you have done, left undone, and hope yet to do. At the same time, it's imperative not to get bogged down in the past.

Mentorship has been one way I seek to give back to others, and philanthropy is another important way to do this. Life Lesson Nine is on this subject:

> On philanthropy my approach is to try to relieve pain rather than spread joy. Music, theater, and art museums have many affluent supporters, give the best parties, and can add to your social luster in a community. They don't need you. Social services, hospitals, and educational institutions can make the world a better place and help the disadvantaged make their way toward the American dream.

Many people are charitable, and when a friend sends me an invitation to a benefit or solicits me for money for a cause, I always try to give at least a small nominal sum. And if it's a close friend or a cause I'm particularly sympathetic to, I try to give more. But when you make a considerable amount of money, you must identify the charities, organizations, and causes where you're willing to commit meaningful amounts of capital.

FINDING FULFILLMENT
THROUGH PHILANTHROPY

Philanthropy has been a deeply fulfilling endeavor, allowing me to give back to the institutions and causes that have profoundly influenced my life. My contributions to education, medical research, and historical preservation are driven by a desire to support and perpetuate the values that shaped my personal and professional journey.

I believe that my education at Harvard College has played a significant role in my success, so I have helped to establish two professorships there: one in drama (the Byron and Anita Wien Professor of Drama) and one in life sciences (the Max and Anne Wien Professor of Life Sciences). The latter can vary in specific fields, and the holder currently focuses on stem cell research. But when that professor retires, it may be in whatever is on the leading edge in life sciences at that time. These gifts feel meaningful to me because my education was so influential in my life. I have also donated a significant amount of money to HBS, which has also contributed meaningfully to my education and subsequent career successes, especially through the relationships I made there.

I've established several scholarships, one in honor of my good friend Don Pritzker, who passed away at thirty-nine and loaned me the money to make my first trip to Europe. These scholarships go to foreign students who intend to return to their developing countries after they graduate. Additionally, I've given a substantial amount to Memorial Sloan Kettering, which has been instrumental in addressing my evolving cancer issues.

I also support the New-York Historical Society (NYHS) because I believe that a sense of history fortifies everyone's ability to understand political developments and cope with a changing world. These contributions are deeply fulfilling because they help perpetuate the values and institutions that have been pivotal in my own life.

Strategic and Impactful Giving

Effective philanthropy requires a strategic approach to ensure meaningful and lasting impact. By leveraging matching grants and providing professional expertise, I have sought to encourage collective giving and support initiatives that promote community development and sustainability.

My serious philanthropy began in the 1980s with the Ackerman Institute, introduced to me by Edwina Brokaw. The organization needed financial stability, so I set up a one-million-dollar matching grant and encouraged other board members to match it collectively. This effort temporarily ensured the institute's viability and demonstrated the power of strategic giving in rallying collective support.

I was also involved with the Volunteer Consulting Group, an offshoot of the Harvard Business School Club of New York, where HBS graduates advised minority businesses. My involvement there was more about active participation than financial contribution, but it underscored the importance of offering professional expertise to support community development.

Leadership and Collaboration in Philanthropy

Leadership and collaboration are essential components of successful philanthropic efforts. Aligning values with organizational missions and forming strategic partnerships have enabled me to help transform institutions and amplify the impact of my contributions.

I served on the board of the Manhattan Institute, brought on by friends Rick Reiss and Walter Mintz as a liberal balance to the conservative thinking on the board. Despite eventually resigning due to differing political philosophies, this experience highlighted the importance of aligning leadership and donor values in nonprofit success. Effective leadership and a shared vision are crucial in steering philanthropic efforts toward meaningful impact.

My work with the NYHS is particularly notable. When the organization was struggling, a conversation with philanthropist Dick Gilder led to his donation of significant historical documents. This, combined with the society's existing collection, formed the largest compilation outside the Library of Congress. Our collaboration brought transformative changes, taking the NYHS from a struggling institution to a thriving one. This experience underscores how strategic partnerships and effective leadership can amplify the impact of philanthropy.

Adapting to Challenges and Ensuring Legacy

Philanthropy must be resilient and adaptable to navigate challenges and ensure a lasting legacy. By maintaining a forward-thinking mindset and continuously supporting growth and innovation, I strive to sustain and expand the impact of my philanthropic endeavors.

Like many institutions, the NYHS faced challenges during COVID-19, affecting attendance and operations. Continuous efforts in fundraising and leadership have kept it resilient. My ongoing support and contributions from others have helped the organization adapt and plan for future expansions, including an ambitious extension on our Central Park West location.

Several years ago, my wife Anita and I were honored by Prep for Prep, an educational nonprofit where Anita has served on the board for many years. During the event, I told the graduates, "Never look back; always be looking forward." This philosophy applies at any stage of life and reflects the forward-thinking mindset essential in both personal and philanthropic endeavors. Adapting to challenges and maintaining a vision for the future are crucial for sustaining and growing philanthropic efforts.

Continue to Add Value

I believe I still have valuable insights to share through my writings, presentations, and perspectives on global events. It would be a disservice to myself and those who invested in my development to stop contributing when I still have something meaningful to offer. With nearly sixty years of experience in finance and investment strategy, I continue to add value by recognizing patterns and trends that may elude less-experienced professionals and by maintaining intellectual flexibility in response to changing economic conditions.

As the senior investment strategist at Blackstone, I regularly share my views on "BXTV" and write essays for internal and client distribution. For instance, my recent analysis of emerging market trends was instrumental in guiding our investment strategy, resulting in significant returns for our clients. Additionally, I often present at industry conferences, where my perspectives help shape broader market discussions.

I feel it's my duty to pass on my knowledge and experiences to the next generation, helping them discover and develop their own talents. One of my most rewarding mentorship experiences was with a young analyst who later became a leading strategist at a major investment firm. Seeing their growth and success affirmed the importance of nurturing talent.

Ensuring that my work and discoveries live on through those I mentor is the most impactful legacy I can leave. Rather than seeking personal accolades, I aim to empower others to carry forward and build upon my life's work, thereby multiplying its impact. By coaching the next generation, I want to create a ripple effect where my insights and approaches continue to evolve and influence the industry long after I am gone.

My philosophy on legacy is not about statues or named buildings but about the people whose lives and careers I have touched. Having several people who deeply impact and carry forward my life's work, continuing to iterate and improve upon it, is the best and most meaningful legacy of all. Through mentorship and sharing knowledge, I strive to ensure that my contributions have a lasting, positive impact on the world.

AFTERWORD

BY TAYLOR BECKER

As you reach the end of this memoir, I hope you have found Byron Wien's stories as enlightening and inspiring as I do. Each chapter, from "Find Your Big Idea" to "Building a Legacy," is filled with practical advice and deep insights that reflect the learnings from Byron's long life and storied career. This afterword aims to distill those lessons and provide you with some actionable steps to incorporate them into your own life.

FINDING YOUR "BIG IDEA"

Byron's career was defined by his ability to identify and pursue transformative ideas. His curiosity and relentless pursuit of knowledge allowed him to stay ahead of trends and make significant contributions to the field of investment strategy. To find your own "big idea," stay curious and open-minded. Challenge conventional wisdom and continuously seek out new information. Embrace the unknown and allow your passions to guide you toward opportunities that align with your strengths and interests.

Finally, be willing to stick your neck out for what you believe in, even, and perhaps especially, when it comes at personal risk to yourself.

If you push the envelope and come up with radical or innovative ideas in your career, you will inevitably experience pushback. Do not shy away from that. Stand up for your ideas, and don't be afraid to lose someone's support or respect. This is invariably harder when you are younger and more junior in your career. Do it anyway (respectfully), and if you are in a place that values intellectual freedom and unconventional thinking, you should be rewarded in time. If you're not, or if doing this impedes your advancement, consider whether you are in the right place for your own long-term personal and professional development.

EVOLVE EACH YEAR

Byron believed in the importance of constant evolution. He never stopped learning and adapting, which kept him relevant and influential throughout his career. Make it a point to evolve each year by setting new goals, learning new skills, and embracing change. Whether through formal education, personal projects, hobbies, or exploring new industries, ensure that you are continually growing and improving.

Life is too short to be complacent. I daresay no one of import has advanced to the top of their respective ladder by remaining stagnant or resistant to change.

NURTURE YOUR NETWORK

One of Byron's most valuable assets was his network. He cultivated relationships with diverse individuals, from industry leaders to young professionals, always valuing what he could learn from others. Invest time in building and maintaining your network. Attend industry events, engage in meaningful conversations, and be genuinely interested in the success of others. Remember that networking is not just about what you can gain but also about how you can contribute and support those around you.

There's an old trope that "it's not what you know; it's *who* you know." That's a bit simplistic. Factual knowledge and expertise are, of course, incredibly important if you are going to be good at your chosen vocation. But there is something profoundly true about the fact that in many industries—maybe in all of them—having robust connections is critical for career progression. Not everyone is fortunate enough to attend prestigious universities or land their first job at a firm that is considered to be best-in-class. Byron's life and mine are evidence of the power of smart networking. Make the cold call. Be warm and generous in your interactions with others. Treat people like friends from the start. Assume good intentions. You will reap the benefits, both personally and professionally.

THERE'S A PERFECT JOB FOR EVERYONE

Byron's journey is a testament to the belief that there is a perfect job for everyone. He found roles that matched his skills and fueled his passions. Reflect on what excites you, and pursue careers that align with those interests. Don't settle for a job that doesn't bring you fulfillment. Be patient and persistent in your search, and don't be afraid to take risks to find your perfect role.

One of Byron's lessons that is easy to roll one's eyes at is his admonition to take the job that is most interesting, not the one that pays the most. "Sure," I can hear certain readers muttering, "that's easy for you to say!" I imagine them picturing Byron with a monocle and top hat, à la the Monopoly Man. (Which is funny for anyone who knew Byron, who was among the most frugal and unostentatious people I have ever known.) It's worth noting, though, that Byron came from very modest means and rose the ranks in his career because of his willingness to find what excited him and to pursue it relentlessly. I am guilty of making life decisions based on cold calculations around my finances, and I can't say any of them were the best decisions I've made. I adhere strongly to the notion that if you aren't passionate about what you do, you'll never "shoot the lights out," so to speak. Pursue what you love, and the money will follow. If it doesn't, it's hard to imagine that the counterfactual scenario would have been worth it, anyway.

COMPASS FOR INVESTORS

Byron's investment philosophy was built on thorough research, critical thinking, and a willingness to embrace unconventional ideas. For those in the investment field, develop your own compass by staying informed about global trends, continuously questioning assumptions, and being open to diverse perspectives. Apply these principles not only to investing but also to all areas of decision-making in your life.

Personally, determining when we have gathered "enough" information to make a decision is one of the most challenging pieces of advice to follow. This difficulty is compounded by the fallacy of information bias, where excessive data accumulation can create a false sense of confidence in our decisions. Recognizing when to stop gathering information and take action is crucial to avoid paralysis by analysis. This is easier said than done, and it's something I strive to get better at. But it brings to light the importance of intellectual humility and of bold decision-making. Embracing the balance between sufficient knowledge and decisive action is key to navigating complex decisions with confidence and clarity.

NEVER RETIRE

Byron's "never retire" mantra reflects his belief in staying active and engaged throughout life. Retirement, for him, meant stepping away from the formal workforce. For others, it might simply mean giving up on the pursuit of meaningful work or other pursuits. Identify what drives you and continue to pursue it with vigor, regardless of age. Staying mentally and physically active will bring you personal satisfaction and allow you to contribute to society in meaningful ways.

Byron's Life Lesson suggested that if you work forever, you can live forever. The biological evidence, unfortunately, remains in opposition to this maxim. Personally, I'm banking on Elon Musk coming up with a solution. But if he doesn't, there is still something very important to take away here. I firmly believe that we start dying the day we stop putting ourselves at risk, whether it's professionally, personally, or intellectually. Never retire from taking risks in your life.

BUILDING YOUR LEGACY

Finally, a key lesson from Byron's life is that one's legacy is much more than the sum of one's personal accomplishments. Success is not just about reaching the top but also about the continuous pursuit of growth, the relationships you build, and the cumulative impact you've had on others.

When our stories are told one day, I believe we will be remembered as much for our mentorship, warmth, and generosity as we will for our career milestones or lifetime earnings. Mentor those who are coming up behind you, share your knowledge, and give back to the organizations and institutions that shaped and helped you along the way.

Thank you for taking the time to read Byron's story. I hope it will help you navigate your own journey in taking risks, embracing change, and living a life of purpose and impact.

APPENDIX

BYRON WIEN PRESENTS "TOP LESSONS FROM AN INVESTING MENTOR"

Byron Wien | Barron's Online | May 2016

There will be no essay on The Smartest Man in Europe this year. My good friend and mentor Edgar de Picciotto, chairman of Union Bancaire Privée in Geneva, has passed away; he was eighty-six. I met him during the 1980s when I was at Morgan Stanley, and he was a regular attendee at our global client conference at Lyford Cay in the Bahamas.

I came to know him well when we were both supervisory directors of Soros Fund Management and met for several days twice a year in Europe. (Soros was an offshore fund.) When I started writing about him in 2002, I chose not to reveal his name to protect his privacy. I did, however, have a shirt made with the legend "Smartest Man in Europe" and gave it to him, but he told me he only wore it around his swimming pool.

Over the years I learned that he didn't think like other investors, and I wondered about the formative events in his background. He was descended from a mercantile family whose roots stretch back hundreds of years to the days when they operated canteens along the Silk Route, providing food and weather protection to travelers moving to and from China and India. Born in Lebanon and educated in Europe, he came to the United States for training in finance. Sensing great opportunity as Europe recovered from World War II, he settled in Geneva and began managing the wealth that was accumulating on the continent. He was an early investor in hedge funds and his reputation as a person who could identify secular change, talent, and undervalued assets ahead of others grew over the years.

He lived well. His homes in and near Geneva contained paintings by artists ranging from Canaletto to Kandinsky. He bought one of the few private homes designed by Oscar Niemeyer (the architect of Brasília). It had fallen into a derelict state, but it was on an incomparable spit of land in St. Jean Cap Ferrat in the south of France, and Edgar restored it impeccably. At its entrance he installed a fuchsia Jeff Koons balloon dog, twenty-five feet tall, which was brought in by crane.

While he took pleasure in his material possessions, it was discussing and reading about ideas that really aroused his enthusiasm. He was one of the first people to identify the investment potential of Japan in the 1980s and then sold his positions before the sharp decline in that market. Before the Berlin Wall came down and Russia began to dismantle its command economy, he saw the changes brewing there and the potential available to domestic and overseas investors. He was an early investor in the emerging markets, and he sold his positions there in a timely way as well. He did the same with gold and technology. After September 11, 2001, he was an aggressive buyer of US stocks, but by the middle of the decade, he cooled, sensing a pending recession.

He pressed upon me the importance of understanding the macro environment. "Many people describe themselves as stock pickers," he would say, "but you have to consider the economic, social and political context in which the stocks are being picked." He encouraged me to meet as many people of influence as I could. For him, networking never stopped. He would test his ideas on those he respected, and if he ran into a strong opposing opinion, he would reflect on it seriously and sometimes change his position. While he never lacked conviction about his ideas, he was open-minded and flexible. "Nobody owns the truth," he would tell me.

As I look back on the titles of my essays about him over the last fifteen years, they provide a chronicle of the market's glory days and pitfalls. In my first essay about him in June 2002, nine months after the attacks on the World Trade Center, he was "upbeat." He believed that although terrorism was a continuing threat to investors and an incident could destabilize markets for a period of time, the world economy was huge and had plenty of momentum, so he was very positive.

Some of what he said in 2002 rings especially true today. "All the portfolio managers I know in America are complaining about how hard it is to make money. No powerful themes are emerging that they can put big money into. The only way to perform is to trade, but the friction costs are great. Portfolio managers in New York still don't understand the importance of global interdependence." So, when many investors were still cautious, he said, "I see an opportunity to make some serious money here: I bought gold on leverage, sold the dollar short, put money in European hedge funds, and invested heavily in Russia. I am excited and very busy and I expect to make a killing." And he did.

In 2003 he talked about the opportunities in China "which is on its way to becoming the manufacturer of everything the world wants, but, as it moves up the technology scale, it will seek political influence. The US is abdicating its political and economic leadership position. You Americans think of yourselves as the brains of the world. You cannot provide jobs for your 300 million people as a service organization. Nine-tenths of your population simply cannot find gainful employment cutting the grass, doing the laundry, and cleaning the houses of the one-tenth that the world holds in awe."

In 2004 Edgar was down on Europe and the United States but bullish on Asia where he saw an expanding middle class. At that time he was beginning to understand the importance of monetary policy in determining the future course of stock and bond prices. He suspected that even though the Fed was likely to be accommodative, inflation was going to stay low, despite the theories of Milton Friedman of the University of Chicago.

In 2005 he was bullish on bonds because of the build-up in liquidity around the world. Few people expected interest rates on US government paper to decline as much as he did. He thought US stocks would do well as a result. He was, however, worried about the debt accumulation taking place at the government, corporate, and individual levels. In 2006 he was focused on the migration of economic opportunity from Europe and the United States to Asia, and the prospect of stagflation in the mature developed countries, but he was still bullish on the United States. He sensed a movement to the left in America (he should have lived to see Bernie Sanders), but he didn't think it would undermine the capitalist spirit of the country. He was positive on India and concerned about the rise of Islam. He was buying gold.

By 2007 he was growing cautious. The title of my essay that year was "The Smartest Man Is Wearing Rain Gear." The title in 2008 was "Overcoat Time for the Smartest Man." He was nervous about the debt incurred by marginal borrowers to buy assets that he considered overvalued. As a result, he pulled out of all the hedge funds where he was locked up beyond one year. By 2008 he was recommending cleansing the US economic system through bankruptcies and a devaluation of the dollar to revive manufacturing, but said that America was not ready to go through a period of severe pain. In any case, he expected the standard of living to remain flat in the West and rise in Asia. He was beginning to cool on globalization.

In 2009 he was bullish again because of the sharp sell-off in world markets. He did caution correctly that growth would only be 2 percent. While he was positive on the US and Europe, he thought there would be stronger growth in Brazil, Russia, India, and China. In 2010 he was worried that the debt in the UK and the US had reached a point where the problem could only be cured by fiscal discipline or inflation or a combination of the two. He thought warning signals would be higher interest rates and inflation, but so far we had not seen either. He was cautious in 2011, and his only investments were in Swiss francs and gold. He was still talking about the high level of government debt everywhere, the possible decline of the dollar, and the uncertain stability of the European Union. He continued to be positive on China and India.

Edgar suggested a title for the 2012 essay: "Dancing Around the Fire of Hell." I paraphrased it, but his view that year was that the debt problems were still there, even though various governments had figured out a way to postpone their consequences. He complained that too many investors think "incrementally," without looking at the broad range of problems facing the markets. He was troubled about Greece but thought its problems were indicative of flawed financial planning everywhere. He anticipated higher interest rates and inflation. He owned a few stocks like Apple and IBM, and had some gold and energy investments.

In 2013 he was bullish on Europe, which was a very contrarian idea at the time. He was impressed with the operating efficiencies that had been put in place by European companies. He had sold his gold and was cool on emerging markets. He was concerned about the Middle East and the confused policy approach of the United States in that region. He was buying Yahoo and Google because of the possibility of open-ended earnings. By 2014 he was totally committed to innovation stocks, believing they represented a new industrial revolution; that theme continued in 2015. He did not expect the markets in Europe and the United States to do much, but he continued to believe technology offered opportunity. He thought governments around the world had proven ineffective at problem solving. His conclusion in 2015 was that there were more risks than opportunities, but you could still make money in technology and biotechnology.

My purpose in reviewing Edgar's thinking over the past fifteen years is to show how he consistently tried to integrate his world view into the investment environment. That was his imperative. He wasn't always right, but he was always questioning himself and he remained flexible. When he lost money, it tended to cause minimal pain in relation to his overall assets, and when one of his maverick ideas worked, he made what he called "serious money."

Edgar was a mentor for me. Over the years I've learned that mentors fall into two categories. There are those you work with every day who are continuously guiding you to improved performance. The late Barton Biggs, my colleague at Morgan Stanley, falls into that category. He developed the concept of impressionistic strategy, writing his essays in the first person as though he was in a conversation with investors rather than in a totally objective style similar to an academic paper. He was totally devoted to his work and he never wasted time. He would take an hour out of each day to exercise, and he loved sports like tennis, golf, and touch football, but when he wasn't exercising, he was reading and writing, and his output included essays and two books with a third in process when he passed away.

The second type of mentor is one whom you see intermittently. These individuals provide guidance because of who they are and what they do. Edgar fell into that category, and I am forever grateful to him for what he taught me. He was fond of breaking rules. Suspicious of diversification as the hiding ground for those without conviction, he believed in concentration: if he liked a country, a sector, or an asset class he was willing to put considerable money into it and exclude representation in other areas more popular with institutional investors. He sought high rewards and was willing to tolerate high risk in the process, once buying an office building in Iraq and selling it a short time later after it had doubled. He was not a trader, but he knew that a good investment had three phases: the period when you are waiting for an offbeat, but promising, idea to work; the period when everyone agrees with you and the stock or asset performs well; and the final period when the asset may still be appreciating but it is time to look for something else because the additional gains will be small. It can be dangerous to overstay a position. I still have not learned this lesson. He was particularly skillful at selling his mistakes quickly. Happily, I have learned that lesson.

But he taught me much more. He took great pleasure from knowing smart people and exchanging ideas with them. In the Morgan Stanley days when Steve Roach our head economist and I would come to Geneva, he would organize a dinner for us at his home and invite a dozen of the leaders of the Swiss financial community to discuss the important issues of the day with us. The Benchmark lunches that I put together in the Hamptons each summer are an outgrowth of this. He taught me to look at houses and objects of art as permanent possessions, not items to be sold at some point. I should buy them because they would enrich my life and I should not sell them because they had appreciated in value, because then I would be parting unnecessarily with something I loved and there would be emptiness as a result. My heirs could do the selling.

He taught me the value of trust and the joy of friendship and the futility of envy. He was proud of his own success but also an admirer of the success of others who were his friends. He never talked about missed opportunities except when he was criticizing himself. He was his own toughest critic, and he encouraged me to be the same. Even if you are an intelligent risk taker, you will make many mistakes. Recognize them early, but never stop taking risks, because that is where the real opportunities are, and your life will be more stimulating as a result.

Edgar enjoyed his cigars and his 1982 Bordeaux collection and his circle of influential people. He worked at the bank until the end because that was the way he could enjoy each day as much as possible. My life is better as a result of having known him and I will always be grateful for that. He wrote a book about his life and called me one day to ask me to write the foreword to it, which I did. Afterward he wrote me a thank you note that I quote here.

"I am grateful for what you have written. I do not deserve your nice words as my professional life has been directed to give the best of my capabilities."

"It was nice that you accepted to write and realize the friendship and feelings you have towards me. I do value your qualities and feel proud of having you as a friend." He was modest and generous to the end. Every mentor should follow his lead.

MORGAN STANLEY

U.S.
Investment
Research

December 28, 1992

Strategy   *Byron R. Wien (212) 703-6256*

The Ten Surprises of 1993

By now everyone seems to be speculating on the unexpected events that will have an impact on investment performance during the year ahead. We suspect that the consensus is already a part of the current price of most stocks, so our future success will come, we think, from correctly calculating how the prevailing views may prove wrong. Back in 1986 when I worked out my first list of ten surprises, I thought of the exercise as an amusing and whimsical way to start the year. Today I have more respect for the process — in fact, the surprises form the foundation of my investment strategy at the start of each year.

Over time, I have derived a procedure for constructing the surprises. During November and December I talk with about 100 portfolio managers in the United States, Europe, and Japan to identify the major investment issues on which a popular perception has formed. My definition of a surprise is an event that is expected by fewer than one-third of the managers I survey. To make my list, each one must meet two important tests. First, the surprise must have investment significance. If it takes place, markets — or at least stocks — must undergo an important change in price. Most critical, the surprise must have, in my opinion, a greater than 50% probability of taking place. Although these are not outright predictions, I believe they are likely events, and I hold myself accountable for them during the course of the year.

It isn't that difficult to come up with a list of surprises. Many Wall Street observers do. Other attempts invariably include an earthquake in California or the discovery of a cure for AIDS and/or cancer. The difference between my list and others is that I think my surprises have a good chance of happening, and I adjust my model portfolio accordingly. This is not an exercise performed simply for the fun of it. To keep the pressure on, I put the surprises on page one of my presentation handout all year, so portfolio managers can have a laugh or two at my expense as the year unfolds. In years when the muse has left me, this discipline has had its painful moments.

If one-third of the surprises take place, they are working out as might be expected. Anything better than that makes me feel that I've had some useful insight. Over the years, I've gotten about 50–60% of the surprises right. In 1991 over 70% were essentially correct, and I appeared on "Wall Street Week" on the first Friday of 1992 to present the surprises for the coming year. That kind of exposure usually means you're headed for trouble, but the results weren't too bad after all. Unlike past years when I have done the grading myself, I submitted the 1992 list to several very smart and very skeptical observers. They graded each surprise on a scale of ten. Of a possible score of 100, I received a 63, leaving me inspired enough to pursue this year's list. Here's a brief review of last year's results:

• I missed the biggest political surprise of all — Ross Perot. I expected something unusual to happen in the course of the presidential election, but I thought it would be that Bush would dump Quayle and go on to win. I didn't expect Perot to announce, tap deeply into the American spirit, withdraw, join the battle again, and end up with 20% of the vote. While the enormous success of the Clinton campaign was certainly a surprise, it was not one I anticipated in December 1991.

• My hunch that the economy would improve noticeably in the second quarter proved too optimistic, but third quarter real gross domestic product was better than consensus expectations, and the fourth quarter looks as if it will end up relatively strong as well.

• At the beginning of 1992, most observers expected the long U.S. Treasury bond yield to drop below 7% from its then level of 7.4%. I thought that the near-term direction of long rates would be up, perhaps as high as 8.5%. That proved too pessimistic, but the long bond did reach an 8.11% yield in the spring, confounding those who were bullish on bonds at the beginning of the year.

• I expected the economies of Western Europe and Japan to move toward recession during 1992. At the beginning of last year, most thought that Europe would expand faster than the United States and that Japan would slow down somewhat but maintain a reasonable growth pace. I thought interest rates would drop in both Europe and Japan and they have, but not to the degree I expected. I also thought the dollar would do well against the mark and the yen. It started the year weakly but is now doing much better against the Deutsche mark. Currently, most portfolio managers expect the relative strength of the U.S. currency to continue, which is a major difference from a year ago.

• At the beginning of last year, Boris Yeltsin had been heading the former Soviet Union for less than five months, and most portfolio managers believed political chaos was around the corner. A year later Yeltsin is still at the helm, as I expected; while his control is not as tight as he would like and reforms have slowed, there has been no upheaval yet. Perhaps the big surprises in that part of the world are yet to come.

• The market did not do as poorly early in the year as I expected, but it did approach the Dow Jones 3500 level by the end of the year, part of my sixth surprise. While a number of active managers had trouble beating the market at the beginning of the year, performance picked up after

October. I had expected most managers to outperform the market in 1992.

• My thinking on inflation was all wrong. I thought the pickup in the economy would move prices higher, but I clearly underestimated how much stuff of all kinds is being produced around the world these days. Intense competition in basic materials markets as well as in manufactured goods is keeping inflation low. And service sector restructuring is starting to have a beneficial impact on the pricing of many services. These trends seem likely to continue. I got a zero on this one, as if I had hit the board during a dive.

• My best surprise was that market leadership would change from the consumer nondurable growth stocks like foods and drugs toward economy-sensitive issues. I thought Congress would focus hard on health care costs, and Clinton's campaign rhetoric suggests that it will. I also thought food companies would lose their pricing power somewhat during 1992. The strength in cyclicals and financials was most pronounced in the first four months of last year, but I think large-capitalization consumer stocks will underperform again in 1993.

• I thought the Japanese market was unprepared for the slowdown I expected there, and I warned that the Nikkei 225 could drop to 15,000. It actually went below that level but has rallied since.

• Finally, I thought the Mexican Miracle would end with a major correction in that market. While an important decline (from above 19,000 to below 13,000, or more than 30%) did occur, the Mexican market is still higher than it was at the start of 1992, and most savvy investors who follow that part of the world expect Mexico to have another good year in 1993.

So much for the Surprises of 1992. Now, let's take a look at this year's list.

1. German interest rates stay high during the first six months of 1993, depriving that country and most of Western Europe of an opportunity to recover from a serious recession. Helmut Schlesinger defends the Bundesbank's position by saying that in the long run his policies will be seen as wise. European markets ignore this hard-line rhetoric and rally in spite of the weak economies there.

MORGAN STANLEY 3

2. United States economic growth is stronger than expected, with GDP expansion exceeding 3%. Employment picks up and the unemployment rate drops to 6.5%, despite fears that an improving economy will produce few new jobs.

3. Bill Clinton pulls back from his tax-the-rich campaign threats, recognizing the need to encourage risk-taking by those who have accumulated capital. He fails to press for an increase in the top personal tax rate to 36%. But he also gives up on reducing the capital gains tax rate, deciding it is too difficult to develop an equitable incentive structure that truly rewards entrepreneurs.

4. Political unrest in the Middle East caused by a continued rise in Islamic fundamentalism leads to a disruption of oil exports. Iran is at the center of the problem. Because of this and an oil import tax that Clinton introduces earlier, the price of West Texas intermediate crude soars to $25.00. Natural gas rises to $3.50 per mcf.

5. In spite of better-than-expected growth in the economy, long-term interest rates decline in the United States. The 30-year U.S. Treasury bond yields less than 7% by midyear. The Dow Jones Industrial average exceeds 4000 early in the year.

6. The combination of a recession and a decline in real estate values in Japan brings the Nikkei 225 to below 10,000.

7. The death of Deng Xiaoping leads to a power struggle in China. Suddenly, geopolitical investment concerns shift to Asia from Europe. Emerging markets along the Pacific Rim decline.

8. Shortly after the inauguration, Clinton's foreign policy skills are tested as the former Soviet Union sells nuclear weapons to an unstable country in order to raise money for food and economic reform. When the new president seems confused and indecisive, his aura fades. Information emerges on questionable past business dealings of two cabinet-level appointees, and the administration loses its legislative momentum.

9. A portfolio of large-cap phoenix stocks outperforms smaller growth issues. IBM ($49) splits into three components. General Motors ($33) and the airlines finally outperform.

10. Although inflation stays low and the former Soviet Union — starved for hard currency — continuously sells bullion, the price of gold rises to $400. Increasing industrial and jewelry demand and world political uncertainty are reported as the reasons for the move.

I'll discuss these surprises in more detail next week.

Model Portfolio Changes

I am adding 1% positions in **Chiron** ($56) and **Paramount Communications** ($45) to the model portfolio. Buying biotechnology stocks is tough on old-time portfolio managers, particularly those who are negative on drugs in particular and high multiples in general. Chiron has important new products coming out over the next few years for multiple sclerosis, herpes, AIDS, and hepatitis. Our analyst Eric Hecht has a target price of $71, based on discounted earning power three years out. Paramount Communications has had mixed results at the box office over the past two years, but the outlook for 1993 is much better. The stock is currently trading at less than a market multiple, and Alan Kassan has a price target of $57 based on the potential earnings leverage from a rise in PCI's market share in the film business. I am removing 1% positions in Boatmen's Bancshares ($56) and Chicago and Northwestern ($21). I remain constructive on both the banks and the rails, but these two stocks, which have performed adequately, do not have the appreciation potential of the issues I have added. In a fully invested portfolio, something has to go to make room for the more promising alternatives. The cash in the model portfolio remains 1%.

MORGAN STANLEY

Morgan Stanley U.S. Model Portfolio

Constructed and managed by Byron R. Wien in consultation with our analysts

Small- and Medium-Capitalization High Quality Growth (14%)

Company	12/31 Price	EPS 92E	EPS 93E	93E P/E	Div	5 Yr. Proj. Gro.	ROE
American Income (AIH)	24	$2.09	$2.30	10	$0.20	12	27
Arrow Electronics (ARW)	29	1.75	2.20	13	–	15	12
Arrow Int'l (ARRO)	25	0.90	1.07	23	0.08	25	25
BE Aerospace (BEAV)	12	1.04	1.20	10	–	20	21
Chiron (CHIR)	56	(0.20)	0.60	–	–	35	–
Cisco Systems (CSCO)	49	1.80	2.85	17	–	35	44
First Fncl Mgt (FFM)	41	2.20	2.40	17	0.10	18	12
Harley-Davidson (HDI)	38	1.47	1.92	20	–	25	21
Hechinger (HECHA)	10	0.75	1.10	9	0.16	20	10
Info Resources (IRIC)	31	0.90	1.20	26	–	30	16
Int'l Game Tech (IGT)	51	1.05	1.43	36	–	35	22
Medco Cont (MCCS)	38	0.60	0.85	45	0.04	35	11
Novell (NOVL)	28	0.89	1.18	24	–	30	33
Promus (PRI)	55	1.63	2.15	26	–	25	10

Economic Pace Sensitive (43%)

Company	12/31 Price	EPS 92E	EPS 93E	93E P/E	Div	5 Yr. Proj. Gro.	ROE
Aerospace (2% versus S&P 2%)							
Allied-Signal (ALD) (a)	60	$3.95	$4.55	13	$1.00	17	19
Air Freight (1% versus S&P 1%)							
Federal Express (FDX)	54	1.54	3.15	17	–	13	8
Autos (8% versus S&P 2%)							
Chrysler (C) (b)	32	1.45	3.25	10	0.60	5	–
Ford (F) (a)	43	0.35	3.00	14	1.60	5	26
General Motors (GM)	32	(1.50)	2.75	12	1.60	5	–
Goodyear (GT) (a)	68	5.12	6.50	10	1.00	6	6
Capital Goods (3% versus S&P 6%)							
Caterpillar (CAT)	54	(2.15)	2.75	20	0.60	12	15
Joy Technologies (JOY)	12	0.25	1.00	12	–	20	51
Trinova (TNV)	21	0.45	1.50	14	0.68	12	14
Chemicals (5% versus S&P 3%)							
IMC Fertilizer (IFL)	43	3.15	2.00	22	1.08	25	13
Monsanto (MTC)	58	2.90	4.25	14	2.24	9	11
Morton Int'l (MII)	61	3.03	3.75	16	0.96	18	12
Rohm & Haas (ROH)	53	3.25	4.00	13	1.32	13	12
Stepan (SCL)	33	2.85	3.50	9	0.80	10	18
Electronics (5% versus S&P 1%)							
Intel (INTC) (b)	87	4.32	6.00	15	0.40	20	20
Motorola (MOT)	104	4.25	6.00	17	0.76	18	12
Sierra Semi (SERA)	13	0.92	0.90	14	–	35	20
Energy (4% versus S&P 12%)							
Burlington Resources (BR)	40	1.25	1.65	24	0.50	35	9
Texaco (TX)	60	3.50	4.40	14	3.20	9	12
Triton Energy (OIL)	34	(3.19)	(0.50)	–	–	13	–
Western Gas (WGR)	26	1.40	2.00	13	0.20	24	17
Environmental Services (1% versus S&P 2%)							
Chemical Waste (CHW)	20	0.77	1.05	19	0.20	20	16
Papers & Containers (5% versus S&P 2%)							
Int'l Paper (IP)	67	3.30	4.70	14	1.68	9	15
Owens-Illinois (OI)	10	0.78	1.00	9	–	20	23
Scott Paper (SPP)	36	2.20	3.30	11	0.80	10	14
Temple-Inland (TIN)	51	2.80	3.20	16	0.88	9	17
Union Camp (UCC)	46	1.30	2.60	18	1.56	11	17
Railroads & Trucking (4% versus S&P 1%)							
CSX (CSX)	69	4.60	5.45	13	1.52	14	10
Conrail (CRR) (a)	47	2.90	3.55	13	1.10	14	8
Union Pacific (UNP)	58	3.55	4.20	14	1.48	12	16
Steel & Nonferrous Metals (5% versus S&P 1%)							
Asarco (AR) (a)	25	1.25	4.25	6	0.80	NM	8
Bethlehem Steel (BS)	16	(3.00)	1.00	16	–	NM	10
Phelps-Dodge (PD) (a)	48	3.85	5.50	9	1.65	6	15

Interest Sensitive or Stable Growth (41%)

Company	12/31 Price	EPS 92E	EPS 93E	93E P/E	Div	5 Yr. Proj. Gro.	ROE
Airlines (7% versus S&P 1%)							
AMR (AMR) (a)	67	($3.50)	$5.00	13	–	12	11
Delta (DAL) (a)	51	(12.00)	5.00	10	$0.20	12	12
UAL (UAL) (a)	126	(11.80)	10.00	13	–	12	17
USAir (U)	13	(7.30)	1.00	13	–	9	12
Banks & Thrifts (9% versus S&P 4%)							
Bank of New York (BK)	54	4.20	5.30	10	1.52	15	14
BankAmerica (BAC)	46	4.80	5.55	8	1.30	15	17
Bankers Trust (BT)	68	7.90	8.95	8	2.80	12	18
Chemical (CHL) (b)	39	2.85	3.85	10	1.20	12	15
Citicorp (CCI)	22	1.20	2.40	9	–	12	15
NationsBank (NB)	51	3.85	4.65	11	1.60	13	16
Shawmut (SNC)	18	1.00	1.65	11	–	15	15
Beverages, Foods, &Tobacco (3% versus S&P 10%)							
Interstate Bakeries (IBC)	19	1.57	1.75	11	0.48	12	16
Philip Morris (MO)	77	5.45	6.50	12	2.60	19	38
RJR Percs (RNPrP)	10	0.62	0.90	11	0.83	10	–
Drugs (1% versus S&P 8%)							
Pfizer (PFE)	72	3.16	3.80	19	1.48	19	14
Gaming (1% versus S&P 1%)							
Circus Circus (CIR)	57	2.17	2.60	22	–	25	25
Insurance (5% versus S&P 3%)							
AMBAC (ABK)	43	3.35	3.75	11	0.44	13	13
American Int'l Group (AIG)	116	7.15	8.25	14	0.56	14	13
Chubb (CB)	89	5.75	6.80	13	1.60	15	16
Primerica (PA)	48	5.20	5.50	9	0.80	13	16
Torchmark (TMK)	57	3.55	4.05	14	1.07	15	27
Publishing/Broadcasting (3% versus S&P 2%)							
Time Warner (TWX)	29	(1.36)	(0.94)	–	0.25	–	–
Paramount (PCI)	45	1.97	3.03	15	0.80	12	8
Viacom (VIA)	44	0.55	1.25	35	–	–	18
Retail (8% versus S&P 6%)							
Charming Shoppes (CHRS)	18	0.75	0.93	19	0.08	20	18
Dayton Hudson (DH)	76	5.00	6.00	13	1.52	16	14
Fingerhut (FHT)	30	2.45	2.90	10	0.32	17	16
Food Lion (FDLNB)	8	0.39	0.50	16	0.11	20	21
Kroger (KR)	15	0.85	1.40	11	–	22	NM
Limited (LTD) (a)	27	1.30	1.65	16	0.28	20	25
Toys 'R Us (TOY)	40	1.45	1.75	23	–	20	18
Textile--Apparel Manufacturers (2% versus S&P 1%)							
Burlington Ind (BUR)	14	1.20	1.55	9	–	24	–
Warnaco (WAC)	40	2.10	2.75	15	–	25	–
Utilities--Telephone, Gas & Electric (2% versus S&P 13%)							
MCI Comm (MCIC) (a)	40	2.20	2.50	16	0.10	14	20

Quality, Good Growth (1%)

Company	12/31 Price	EPS 92E	EPS 93E	93E P/E	Div	5 Yr. Proj. Gro.	ROE
Information Processing (1% versus S&P 5%)							
Adobe Systems (ADBE)	31	$2.20	$2.55	12	$0.32	15	35

Cash (1%)

5 year projected growth rate and ROE are normalized
(a) = Weighting 2%
(b) = Weighting 3%
NM = Not Meaningful
A = Actual
E = Estimate

MORGAN STANLEY

**U.S.
Investment
Research**

January 3, 1994

Strategy

Byron R. Wien (212) 703-6256

The Ten Surprises of 1994

Perhaps the biggest surprise of 1993 was that in spite of numerous man-made and natural disasters, including a notable bombing and widespread floods, nothing calamitous happened in the financial markets. All of us would like to be up 70% like the hot hedge-fund operators, but most money managers had respectable performance last year. In the United States, stocks outperformed cash, while bonds did even better. The European stock markets did well although the economies there didn't, and the emerging markets had another year of blockbuster performance. Even Japan was up for the first time in four years.

I think 1994 will be a more turbulent time for investors and that complacency will be the enemy of satisfactory performance. The basic premise for The Ten Surprises is that by anticipating the unexpected and positioning portfolios accordingly, an investor can experience superior performance, since the consensus is already embodied in the price of financial assets. Each year during November and December I talk with about 100 portfolio managers in an attempt to determine the locus of popular perceptions. My definition of a surprise continues to be an event that is expected by no more than one-third of those surveyed.

The surprise must meet two other tests. First, it must have investment significance. Sectors or individual stocks would be expected to undergo a material price change if the event took place. Second, I personally must believe the event has at least a 50% probability of taking place. The surprises

therefore are likely events, in my opinion. While they are not outright predictions, I consider myself accountable for them, and the first page of my client presentation handout always shows the list no matter how humiliating it turns out to be during the course of the year. I also make adjustments in the U.S. model portfolio to reflect my thinking about the surprises. The Ten Surprises have their fans and their detractors, but I must confess that over the years my enthusiasm for the process of developing them has increased. By continuously reflecting on the unexpected, you tend to anticipate change or, at least, be ready for it when it occurs — a mindset that is critical to successful investing.

While it is the process that is most important, I do keep score. At a minimum I should get a 33 out of 100, with each of the ten surprises having a top score of 10. Generally, I end up in the 50 to 60 range. Last year the world-wise and generally unsympathetic review committee gave me scores in the low 60s. Morgan Stanley senior economist Steve Roach came up with something in the low 40s, but you know how economists are with numbers.

Here is my review of the Surprises of 1993. See how you come out.

• My first surprise was that European interest rates would stay higher than expected in the first half of 1993, when almost everyone expected German and French rates to

MORGAN STANLEY

plummet. While rates did gradually come down, they stayed higher than many thought, leaving European economies stuck in a recession. I also expected the European equity markets to do well in spite of weak business conditions and high rates, and that's the way the year developed.

- I expected the U.S. economy to do well last year, but it wasn't until the fourth quarter that it showed strong improvement. I was right that the unemployment rate would drop to 6.5%, although job creation continues to be a key issue for the country and the administration.

- I thought Bill Clinton would soften his line on taxing the rich and retreat from his plan to increase the top personal tax rate. He turned out to be at least as rough on high income earners as anyone feared. Still, he did leave the capital gains rate alone, creating a differential that should favor growth-oriented financial assets. I got little credit for this one.

- At the beginning of last year I was very worried about Moslem fundamentalism as an increasingly important geopolitical issue. I clearly did not anticipate the bombing of the World Trade Center, however, since I had a 2:15 p.m. appointment there on the day of the bombing. My expectation was that the price of oil would rise and energy would be an attractive sector. Energy stocks did well in the first three quarters, but this was a case of being right for the wrong reasons.

- Of all of my 1993 surprises, the most important to have gotten right was the one on U.S. interest rates. I expected long-term Treasury yields to drop to 6.5%, and, as we all happily know, they went below 6%. The decline in interest rates was one of the major driving forces for the U.S. equity market in 1993. I thought, however, that the Dow Jones would do even better than it did. The index did not reach 4000 as I said it might.

- Although the Japanese economy did poorly last year, investors' hope that the Ministry of Finance and the Bank of Japan could develop a plan to improve business conditions in 1994 kept that market from declining sharply. I whiffed this one.

- I also thought there might be instability in China. Even though the government attempted to restrain inflation by

slowing growth, China kept moving forward and remains the most promising investment opportunity in the world today. The emerging markets had another good year despite my worries.

- As I and many others feared, foreign policy proved to be a difficult part of Bill Clinton's on-the-job training. His skill wasn't tested by Soviet plans to sell nuclear weapons as I had indicated, however. More remote places like Bosnia, Somalia, and Haiti caused him greater problems and confusion. I also anticipated that information would emerge on questionable past business dealings of certain cabinet-level appointees, but I didn't think withholding taxes for housekeepers would be the issue.

- I thought that a portfolio of the grand old titans of American industry would be a strong performer, and some of the ones I named, like General Motors ($57) did quite well. They did not outperform smaller growth stocks, however. Perhaps my enthusiasm for the former greats went too far.

- Finally, I thought 1993 would be the year for gold and that its price would exceed $400. It did sell above that level for a while, and I think it will again. Supply and demand will be the important forces behind the move, rather than political instability and inflation.

Here are The Ten Surprises of 1994. They take me further out on a limb than usual, but I think it would be useful for portfolio managers to reflect on the investment implications of each of them. While I am responsible for the surprises, I am indebted to Barton Biggs, Steve Roach, Tom McManus, and numerous clients who offered me counsel and suggestions over the past month.

1. Even without interest rates coming down sharply in France and Germany, the economies of Western Europe recover strongly rather than limping along as most observers expect. Both the mark and the franc are strong against the dollar, and U.S. exports increase markedly, contributing to better-than-expected growth for the American economy as well.

2. Better worldwide growth coupled with disappointing crops in the American Midwest cause a surge in agricultural and industrial commodity prices. Inflation becomes a concern as the Commodity Research Bureau

MORGAN STANLEY

futures index moves above 250. The Fed tightens and the bond market becomes unsettled. Long U.S. Treasuries yield 7.5%. Short rates rise 150 basis points.

3. The combination of continuing strength in the U.S. economy, higher commodity prices, and Fed tightening results in a 15% correction in the American stock market in the first half of 1994. Fears of another 1987 sell-off prove to be unfounded, however.

4. Angry about congressional intransigence, Bill Clinton cancels plans to get his healthcare program passed in 1994. He declares, "The American people are ready for universal healthcare, but their leaders are not." Pharmaceutical, HMO, and medical equipment stocks soar.

5. After the death of Deng Xiaoping, the hard-liners succeeding him present a plan to make Shanghai the financial center of China. As such, they proclaim "1997 means 1997" and indicate that Hong Kong definitely will become a part of the People's Republic at that time. Southeast Asian markets are thrown into turmoil.

6. Frustrated by surveillance and sanctions, Saddam Hussein makes a second hostile foray — this time into southeastern Turkey. The United States provides weapons and planes for Turkey to defend itself against Iraq, but no ground troops. Oil prices rise on fears of a disruption in supply.

7. A military insurrection erupts in Ukraine because of attempts by Moscow to challenge its fragile independence. Natural gas supplies moving to Europe through Ukrainian pipelines for the 1994–95 winter heating season are threatened, leading to higher prices for both gold and oil.

8. Bill Clinton's inability to get his legislative program moving through Congress leads to sharp gains by the Republicans in the November elections, and the GOP becomes the majority party in the Senate. Campaign talk of rolling back Clinton's tax hikes moves the U.S. stock market higher in the summer and fall. The coming year proves to be very volatile.

9. Investors speeding down the information superhighway theme run into a fog-bound patch. Television addicts begin to check into hospitals complaining of stress-related illnesses resulting from too many choices. One critic says these deals make about as much sense as auto manufacturers owning oil companies.

10. A new management style sparks a "we can do it" revolution at IBM ($56). Renewed research into previously abandoned projects yields important new approaches to current computing problems, and profitable opportunities multiply. The stock trades in triple digits once again.

I thought you might be interested in or, in some cases, amused by several of the surprise "also rans."

11. The New York State Employee Retirement Fund requires its managers to have at least some investments in South Africa in recognition of the progress that country is making in dismantling apartheid.

12. Workers of the world unite in their response to mounting global unemployment, confirming one of the basic tenets of a now defunct communism and ushering in an era of social unrest. Robert Reich resigns from the Clinton administration to head up a global pro-labor movement. Ross Perot serves as his fund raiser.

13. The Securities and Exchange Commission becomes concerned about the trading practices of hedge funds and other investment limited partnerships. The commission claims that the leveraged nature of these entities makes them potentially destabilizing to the financial markets. An effort to impose controls is supported by conventional money management firms, which claim they are losing some of their best talent to high-paying partnerships, jeopardizing the future of the nation's retirement system.

14. The U.S. recognizes Cuba and Vietnam, and emerging markets begin to develop there. The feeding frenzy in the Pacific Rim and Latin America subsides, however.

More on this year's surprises next week. Good luck to all of you in the new year.

MORGAN STANLEY

U.S. Model Portfolio Changes

I am adding 1% positions in two stocks to the model portfolio today. The first, IBM ($56), is the subject of my tenth surprise — that the company's profitability is restored more rapidly than many investors anticipate. Steve Milunovich, who rates the stock hold, has said that "the tide has turned psychologically" for Big Blue. If earnings exceed expectations, significant appreciation from current levels could result. I am also adding **Vesta Insurance Group** ($25). Norm Rosenthal likes the company because

it has shown an underwriting profit every year since 1984 in a difficult environment. His target price is $42.

I am removing two 1% positions from the model portfolio. IMC Fertilizer ($45) has increased in price from $27 in September to $45. Les Ravitz believes the stock price fully values the intermediate-term outlook and has reduced his rating to hold. I am also eliminating Warnaco ($30) because the outlook for apparel and retailing looks mediocre unless there is a powerful case for market share gains. The cash in the model portfolio remains 14%.

MORGAN STANLEY

Morgan Stanley U.S. Model Portfolio

Constructed and managed by Byron R. Wien
in consultation with our analysts

Small- and Medium-Capitalization High Quality Growth (13%)

Company	12/31 Price	EPS 93E	EPS 94E	94E P/E	Div	5 Yr. Proj. Gro.	ROE
American Income (AIH)	25	$2.25	$2.55	10	$0.20	12	27
Arrow Electronics (ARW)	42	2.45	2.85	15	–	15	17
Arrow Int'l (ARRO)	24	1.11	1.33	18	0.08	22	25
Family Dollar (FDO)	17	1.22	1.41	12	0.30	15	20
Gilead (GILD)	12	(0.88)	(1.82)	–	0.00	–	–
Harley-Davidson (HDI)	44	1.95	2.35	19	0.24	20	20
Kenetech (KWND)	20	(0.25)	0.45	44	0.00	35	25
Marvel Ent (MRV)	27	0.54	0.73	37	–	22	NM
Merisel (MSEL)	18	0.95	1.35	13	0.00	20	13
Novell (NOVL)	21	0.90	1.10	19	0.00	25	33
Silicon Graphics (SGI)	25	0.70	0.93	27	0.00	27	13
Structural Dynam (SDRC)	14	0.55	0.77	18	0.00	25	12
TBC Tire (TBCC)	12	0.72	0.83	14	0.00	12	22

Economic Pace Sensitive (36%)

Company	12/31 Price	EPS 93E	EPS 94E	94E P/E	Div	5 Yr. Proj. Gro.	ROE
Aerospace (1% versus S&P 2%)							
Grumman (GQ)	40	$3.39	$3.85	10	$1.20	8	15
Air Freight (2% versus S&P 1%)							
Airborne Freight (ABF)	35	1.45	1.75	20	0.30	11	13
Federal Express (FDX)	71	2.90	4.10	17	–	13	8
Autos (8% versus S&P 3%)							
Chrysler (C) (b)	53	5.10	6.70	8	0.80	12	–
Ford (F) (a)	64	4.10	5.25	12	1.60	7	26
General Motors (GM)	55	2.15	4.90	11	0.80	6	–
Goodyear (GT) (a)	46	3.25	3.80	12	0.60	15	6
Capital Goods (2% versus S&P 5%)							
Joy Technologies (JOY)	12	0.40	0.80	15	–	20	51
Tenneco (TGT)	53	2.25	3.55	15	1.60	12	22
Chemicals (3% versus S&P 3%)							
Air Products (APD)	44	2.43	2.73	16	0.92	12	13
Morton Int'l (MII)	94	3.60	5.00	19	1.12	18	13
Rohm & Haas (ROH)	60	2.65	3.15	19	1.40	13	17
Electronics (4% versus S&P 1%)							
Intel (INTC) (b)	62	5.25	5.85	11	0.20	18	20
Motorola (MOT)	92	3.10	3.60	26	0.44	18	12
Energy (8% versus S&P 10%)							
Anadarko (APC)	45	0.98	1.42	32	0.30	15	12
Burlington Res (BR)(a)	42	1.50	1.90	22	0.55	14	9
Mobil (MOB)	79	5.20	5.80	14	3.40	12	12
Occidental (OXY)	17	0.00	0.50	34	1.00	35	6
Triton Energy (OIL)	30	(0.54)	0.50	60	–	16	–
Unocal (UCL)	28	1.40	1.70	16	0.80	25	11
Western Gas (WGR)	33	1.60	2.35	14	0.20	26	17
Papers & Containers (1% versus S&P 2%)							
Weyerhaeuser (WY)	45	2.20	3.20	14	1.20	11	16
Railroads & Trucking (4% versus S&P 1%)							
CSX (CSX)	82	4.55	6.00	14	1.52	14	10
Conrail (CRR) (a)	67	3.55	4.00	17	1.30	14	8
Union Pacific (UNP)	63	3.80	4.50	14	1.60	12	16
Steel & Nonferrous Metals (3% versus S&P 1%)							
Phelps-Dodge (PD) (a)	49	2.60	1.35	36	1.65	–	15
Reynolds Metals (RLM)	45	(1.42)	1.75	26	1.00	–	17

Interest Sensitive or Stable Growth (35%)

Company	12/31 Price	EPS 93E	EPS 94E	94E P/E	Div	5 Yr. Proj. Gro.	ROE
Airlines (6% versus S&P 1%)							
AMR (AMR) (a)	67	($1.00)	$8.00	8	–	12	11
Delta (DAL) (a)	55	(4.35)	4.00	14	$0.20	12	12
UAL (UAL) (a)	146	(2.50)	10.00	15	–	12	17
Banks & Thrifts (10% versus S&P 5%)							
Bank of New York (BK)	57	5.75	6.85	8	1.80	15	16
BankAmerica (BAC)	46	4.75	5.50	8	1.40	12	17
Bankers Trust (BT)	79	10.15	10.15	8	3.12	12	18
BayBanks (BBNK)	51	3.35	4.30	12	1.00	17	15
Chase Manhattan (CMB)	34	3.95	5.00	7	1.20	9	14
Chemical (CHL) (b)	40	4.60	5.50	7	1.32	10	15
Citicorp (CCI)	37	3.30	4.65	8	–	11	15
NationsBank (NB)	49	4.95	5.65	9	1.68	13	16
Beverages, Foods, & Tobacco (1% versus S&P 10%)							
Philip Morris (MO)	56	4.65	5.15	11	2.60	12	38
Communications (3% versus S&P 2%)							
Cisco Systems (CSCO)	65	1.66	2.70	24	–	35	45
MCI Comm (MCIC) (a)	28	1.33	1.52	18	0.05	15	20
Drugs (2% versus S&P 6%)							
Abbott (ABT)	30	1.68	1.87	16	0.68	13	38
Pfizer (PFE)	69	3.75	4.25	16	1.68	16	14
Insurance (5% versus S&P 3%)							
Chubb (CB)	78	6.25	7.25	11	1.72	15	16
Mutual Risk (MM)	30	1.44	1.70	18	0.28	25	20
Primerica (PA)	39	3.53	4.25	9	0.50	13	18
TIG Holdings (TIG)	23	(3.15)	1.50	15	0.20	25	–
Vesta (VTA)	25	1.11	2.32	11	0.20	25	15
Managed Care (1% versus S&P 1%)							
United Health (UNH)	76	2.45	3.05	25	0.03	27	24
Publishing/Broadcasting (4% versus S&P 3%)							
CBS (CBS)	288	17.40	18.00	16	2.00	10	18
Cap Cities/ABC (CCB)	620	28.00	34.65	18	0.20	10	11
Paramount (PCI)	78	2.39	2.82	28	0.80	12	8
Viacom (VIA)	49	0.90	1.10	45	–	–	15
Retail (3% versus S&P 6%)							
Charming Shoppes (CHRS)	12	0.75	1.00	12	0.09	20	22
Fingerhut (FHT)	28	1.48	1.73	16	0.16	18	16
Gap (GPS)	39	1.70	2.10	19	0.40	18	27

Quality, Good Growth (2%)

Company	12/31 Price	EPS 93E	EPS 94E	94E P/E	Div	5 Yr. Proj. Gro.	ROE
Information Processing (2% versus S&P 5%)							
Hewlett-Packard (HWP)	79	$4.80	$4.50	18	$1.00	12	12
IBM (IBM)	56	0.04	2.10	27	1.00	5	12

Cash (14%)

5 year projected growth rate and ROE are normalized
(a) = Weighting 2%
(b) = Weighting 3%
NM = Not Meaningful
A = Actual
E = Estimate

ABOUT THE AUTHORS

BYRON WIEN (1933-2023) was a distinguished market strategist renowned for his annual "Ten Surprises" and "Life's Lessons" lists. He received an AB with honors from Harvard College and an MBA with distinction from Harvard Business School.

Mr. Wien served for twenty-one years as chief US investment strategist at Morgan Stanley. In 1995, he coauthored a book with George Soros: *Soros on Soros—Staying Ahead of the Curve*. He was chief investment strategist for Pequot Capital before joining Blackstone in 2009, where he served as vice chairman in the Private Wealth Solutions group, advising on economic, social, and political trends.

Mr. Wien received numerous accolades, including being named the most widely read analyst on Wall Street by First Call in 1998 and the No. 1 strategist by SmartMoney.com in 2000. He was on the 2004 *Smart Money* Power 30 list and was one of *New York Magazine*'s sixteen most influential people on Wall Street in 2006. The New

York Society of Security Analysts (NYSSA) awarded him a Lifetime Achievement Award in 2008.

He served on the boards and investment committees of many not-for-profit organizations, including the Harvard Volunteer Consulting Group, the Ackerman Institute, Phoenix House, the Manhattan Institute (where he was vice chairman), the Open Society Foundation, Lincoln Center, the Pritzker Foundation, the JPB Foundation, and the New-York Historical Society.

TAYLOR BECKER is an MBA candidate at Harvard Business School. Prior to this, Taylor was a vice president at Blackstone, where he worked on the firm's investment strategy team. In this role, he analyzed global macroeconomic and financial market trends and supported the development of thought leadership that guided asset allocation and investment decisions. Additionally, Mr. Becker advised the firm's investment professionals and other stakeholders on their respective macroeconomic exposures.

Mr. Becker is a member of the Leadership Network at the American Enterprise Institute and the American Council on Germany. He has also served on the Legacy Council at the New-York Historical Society, the Emerging Leaders Council at East Harlem Tutorial Program, and the Junior Committee at the Union League Club of New York.

Mr. Becker received a BA with honors from the University of Pennsylvania in 2017, where he graduated summa cum laude.